Essential Dictionary of Composers

The most practical and useful source available for students and professionals

L. C. HARNSBERGER

Special thanks to:
Jennifer Balue, Kyleen Denney, Joe Stoebenau, the estate of George Gershwin, Fred and Therese Harnsberger and Ron Manus.

COVER ARTWORK:
All portraits except *Woody Guthrie*—Archiv für Kunst und Geschichte, London; *Woody Guthrie*—Culver Pictures, PNI

Book design: Sue Hartman
Cover design: Carol Kascsak, Ted Engelbart

Copyright © MCMXCVII by Alfred Publishing Co., Inc.
All rights reserved.   Printed in USA.

ISBN 0-88284-765-1

The Essential Dictionary of Composers

1. Clara Schumann
2. Johannes Brahms
3. Niccolò Paganini
4. Claudio Monteverdi
5. Ludwig van Beethoven
6. Wolfgang Amadeus Mozart
7. Béla Bartók
8. Scott Joplin
9. Antonio Vivaldi
10. Johann Sebastian Bach
11. Igor Stravinsky
12. Woody Guthrie
13. Franz Schubert
14. Giuseppe Verdi
15. George Gershwin

Names in parentheses are those not commonly used, such as a middle name. Names in brackets are alternate spellings or names which were changed.

A

Adam, Adolphe (Charles)
BORN: July 24, 1803—Paris
DIED: May 3, 1856—Paris
HISTORICAL PERIOD: Romantic
COMPOSITIONAL MEDIA: Opera, ballet, songs.
IMPORTANT ITEMS: Notable works include the ballet "Giselle."

Adams, John (Coolidge)
BORN: February 15, 1947—Worcester, MA
HISTORICAL PERIOD: Modern
COMPOSITIONAL MEDIA: Orchestra, opera, chamber, keyboard, film.
IMPORTANT ITEMS: Composes in the minimalist style. Notable works include the opera "Nixon in China."

Addinsell, Richard (Stewart)
BORN: January 13, 1904—London
DIED: November 14, 1977—London
HISTORICAL PERIOD: Modern
COMPOSITIONAL MEDIA: Songs, film.
IMPORTANT ITEMS: Notable works include the "Warsaw Concerto."

Adler, Richard
BORN: August 3, 1921—New York
HISTORICAL PERIOD: Modern
COMPOSITIONAL MEDIA: Musicals, songs.
IMPORTANT ITEMS: Notable musicals include "Pajama Game" and "Damn Yankees."

Adler, Samuel (Hans)
BORN: March 4, 1928—Mannheim, Germany
HISTORICAL PERIOD: Modern
COMPOSITIONAL MEDIA: Orchestra, chamber music, keyboard, choral, opera, songs.
IMPORTANT ITEMS: Named chairman of the Eastman school of music in 1973. His compositions are inspired by Jewish liturgical music.

Albéniz, Isaac (Manuel Francesco)
BORN: May 29, 1860—Camprodón, Spain
DIED: May 18, 1909—Cambô-les-Bains, France
HISTORICAL PERIOD: Romantic
COMPOSITIONAL MEDIA: Keyboard, orchestra, choral, opera.
IMPORTANT ITEMS: Notable works include the piano suite "Iberia" which was later orchestrated by Enrique Arbós.

Alberti, Domenico
BORN: 1710—Venice
DIED: 1740—Rome
HISTORICAL PERIOD: Late Baroque/Early Classical
COMPOSITIONAL MEDIA: Keyboard, choral, opera.
IMPORTANT ITEMS: His arpeggiated style of keyboard accompaniment is known as "Alberti Bass."

Albinoni, Tomaso (Giovanni)
BORN: June 8, 1671—Venice
DIED: January 17, 1751—Venice
HISTORICAL PERIOD: Baroque
COMPOSITIONAL MEDIA: Opera, chamber music, orchestra.
IMPORTANT ITEMS: Notable works include the "Adagio" for strings and organ and the opera "Griselda."

Anderson, Leroy
BORN: June 29, 1908—Cambridge, MA
DIED: May 18, 1975—Woodbury, CT
HISTORICAL PERIOD: Modern (Popular)
COMPOSITIONAL MEDIA: Orchestra.
IMPORTANT ITEMS: Composer of light instrumental music including "The Syncopated Clock," "Sleigh Ride" and "The Typewriter," all originally composed for the Boston Pops Orchestra.

Antheil, George [Georg] (Johann Carl)
BORN: July 8, 1900—Trenton, NJ
DIED: February 12, 1959—New York
HISTORICAL PERIOD: Modern
COMPOSITIONAL MEDIA: Orchestra, ballet, keyboard, choral, opera, film.
IMPORTANT ITEMS: Caused a furor with compositions, such as "Ballet Mécanique," which incorporates sounds of car horns, anvils and the sound of an airplane.

Arlen, Harold
[real name: Hyman Arluck]
BORN: February 15, 1905—Buffalo, NY
DIED: April 23, 1986—
HISTORICAL PERIOD: Modern (Popular)
COMPOSITIONAL MEDIA: Popular songs, film.
IMPORTANT ITEMS: Notable works include the songs "Stormy Weather" and "Over the Rainbow."

Arnold, Malcolm (Henry)
BORN: October 21, 1921—Northampton, England
HISTORICAL PERIOD: Modern
COMPOSITIONAL MEDIA: Orchestra, chamber music, opera, ballet, songs, film.
IMPORTANT ITEMS: Prolific composer whose film scores include "The Bridge on the River Kwai."

Auric, Georges
BORN: February 15, 1899—Lodève, Hérault, France
DIED: July 23, 1983—Paris
HISTORICAL PERIOD: Modern
COMPOSITIONAL MEDIA: Ballet, film, chamber music, orchestra, songs.
IMPORTANT ITEMS: A member of Les Six.

B

Babbitt, Milton (Byron)
BORN: May 10, 1916—Philadelphia, PA
HISTORICAL PERIOD: Modern
COMPOSITIONAL MEDIA: Orchestra, keyboard, songs, electronic.
IMPORTANT ITEMS: Influential serial composer.

Bach, Carl [Karl] Philipp Emanuel
BORN: March 8, 1714—Weimar, Germany
DIED: December 14, 1788—Hamburg
HISTORICAL PERIOD: Early Classical
COMPOSITIONAL MEDIA: Orchestra, chamber music, keyboard, choral.
IMPORTANT ITEMS: Third (second surviving) son of J.S. Bach. A prolific composer and author of a celebrated treatise on keyboard playing.

Bach, Johann Christian
BORN: September 5, 1735—Leipzig, Germany
DIED: January 1, 1782—London
HISTORICAL PERIOD: Early Classical
COMPOSITIONAL MEDIA: Orchestra, chamber music, keyboard, choral, opera.
IMPORTANT ITEMS: Youngest son of J.S. Bach, who influenced the music of Mozart, Haydn and Beethoven.

Bach, Johann Christoph Friedrich
BORN: June 21, 1732—Leipzig, Germany
DIED: January 26, 1795—Buckeburg, Germany
HISTORICAL PERIOD: Classical
COMPOSITIONAL MEDIA: Orchestra, keyboard, choral, songs.
IMPORTANT ITEMS: Ninth son of J.S. Bach.

Bach, Johann Sebastian
BORN: March 21, 1685—Eisenach, Germany
DIED: July 28, 1750—Leipzig, Germany
HISTORICAL PERIOD: Baroque
COMPOSITIONAL MEDIA: Orchestra, chamber music, keyboard, choral.
IMPORTANT ITEMS: One of the most important and influential composers in the history of music who mastered the composition of contrapuntal music. Some notable works include the sacred cantatas, St. Matthew and St. John Passions, the B-Minor Mass, as well as keyboard works including the Well Tempered Clavier and two- and three-part inventions.

Bach, Wilhelm Friedemann
BORN: November 22, 1710—Weimar, Germany
DIED: July 1, 1784—Berlin
HISTORICAL PERIOD: Early Classical
COMPOSITIONAL MEDIA: Orchestra, chamber music, keyboard, choral.
IMPORTANT ITEMS: Eldest son of J.S. Bach.

Bacharach, Burt
BORN: May 12, 1928—Kansas City, MO
HISTORICAL PERIOD: Modern (Popular)
COMPOSITIONAL MEDIA: Popular songs, film.
IMPORTANT ITEMS: Notable songs include "Raindrops Keep Falling on My Head," "Do You Know the Way to San Jose" and "What the World Needs Now Is Love."

Bacon, Ernst
BORN: May 26, 1898—Chicago, IL
DIED: March 16, 1990—Orinda, CA
HISTORICAL PERIOD: Modern
COMPOSITIONAL MEDIA: Orchestra, songs, chamber music, choral, opera.
IMPORTANT ITEMS: A prolific composer of songs.

Balakirev, Mily Alexeievich
BORN: January 2, 1837—Nizhny-Novgorod
DIED: May 29, 1910—St. Petersburg
HISTORICAL PERIOD: Romantic
COMPOSITIONAL MEDIA: Orchestra, chamber music, keyboard, choral, songs.
IMPORTANT ITEMS: A Russian nationalist composer and member of the Russian Five.

Barber, Samuel
BORN: March 9, 1910—West Chester, PA
DIED: January 23, 1981—New York
HISTORICAL PERIOD: Modern
COMPOSITIONAL MEDIA: Orchestra, chamber music, keyboard, opera, songs.
IMPORTANT ITEMS: Notable works include the orchestral work "Adagio for Strings."

Bartók, Béla
BORN: March 25, 1881—Transylvania
DIED: September 26, 1945—New York
HISTORICAL PERIOD: Modern
COMPOSITIONAL MEDIA: Orchestra, chamber music, ballet, keyboard, choral.
IMPORTANT ITEMS: Collector of Hungarian folk music with Kodály. Notable works include "Concerto for Orchestra" and "Music for Strings, Percussion and Celesta."

Bassett, Leslie (Raymond)
BORN: January 22, 1923—Hanford, CA
HISTORICAL PERIOD: Modern
COMPOSITIONAL MEDIA: Orchestra, chamber music, keyboard, choral, electronic.
IMPORTANT ITEMS: Awarded the Pulitzer Prize in 1966 for his "Variations for Orchestra."

Beach, Amy (Marcy)
[maiden name: Cheney]
BORN: September 5, 1867—Henniker, NH
DIED: December 27, 1944—New York
HISTORICAL PERIOD: Romantic
COMPOSITIONAL MEDIA: Songs, chamber music, choral, orchestra, keyboard.
IMPORTANT ITEMS: One of the first important American woman composers.

Beethoven, Ludwig van
BORN: December 16, 1770—Bonn, Germany
DIED: March 26, 1827—Vienna
HISTORICAL PERIOD: Classical
COMPOSITIONAL MEDIA: Orchestra, chamber music, keyboard, choral, opera.
IMPORTANT ITEMS: One of the most important composers in the history of music. Despite gradual hearing loss and eventual complete deafness in 1819, he composed until his death. Notable works include nine symphonies, the "Moonlight Sonata" and "Für Elise" for piano and the "Missa Solemnis."

Bellini, Vincenzo
BORN: November 3, 1801—Catania, Sicily
DIED: September 23, 1835—Puteaux, France
HISTORICAL PERIOD: Romantic
COMPOSITIONAL MEDIA: Opera, chamber music, choral.
IMPORTANT ITEMS: Notable works include the opera "Norma."

Bennett, Richard Rodney
>BORN: March 29, 1936—Broadstairs, Kent, England
>HISTORICAL PERIOD: Modern
>COMPOSITIONAL MEDIA: Opera, orchestra, chamber music, vocal, film, TV, keyboard.
>IMPORTANT ITEMS: Prolific composer who incorporates atonality and jazz with traditional harmony and structures.

Bennett, Robert Russell
>BORN: June 15, 1894—Kansas City, MO
>DIED: August 17, 1981—New York
>HISTORICAL PERIOD: Modern
>COMPOSITIONAL MEDIA: Orchestra, chamber music, keyboard, choral, opera, songs, film, band.
>IMPORTANT ITEMS: Notable works include orchestrations of Broadway musicals including "My Fair Lady."

Berg, Alban
>BORN: February 9, 1885—Vienna
>DIED: December 24, 1935—Vienna
>HISTORICAL PERIOD: Modern
>COMPOSITIONAL MEDIA: Orchestra, chamber music, keyboard, opera, songs.
>IMPORTANT ITEMS: A student of Arnold Schoenberg whose compositions incorporate twelve-tone techniques. Notable works include the opera "Wozzeck."

Berio, Luciano
>BORN: October 24, 1925—Oneglia, Italy
>HISTORICAL PERIOD: Modern
>COMPOSITIONAL MEDIA: Orchestra, chamber music, ballet, keyboard, choral, electronic.
>IMPORTANT ITEMS: Compositions incorporate graphic notation and quotes from works of other composers.

Berlin, Irving
>BORN: May 11, 1888—Temun, Russia
>DIED: September 22, 1989—New York
>HISTORICAL PERIOD: Modern (Popular)
>COMPOSITIONAL MEDIA: Popular songs.
>IMPORTANT ITEMS: Notable songs include "Alexander's Ragtime Band," "White Christmas" and "God Bless America."

Berlioz, Hector
>BORN: December 11, 1803—La-Cote-Saint-André, Isère
>DIED: March 8, 1869—Paris
>HISTORICAL PERIOD: Romantic
>COMPOSITIONAL MEDIA: Orchestra, choral, opera.
>IMPORTANT ITEMS: Use of the orchestra was ahead of his time, as seen in the composition "Symphonie Fantastique."

Bernstein, Elmer
>BORN: April 4, 1922—New York
>HISTORICAL PERIOD: Modern
>COMPOSITIONAL MEDIA: Film, chamber music, musicals, orchestra, songs.
>IMPORTANT ITEMS: Notable film scores include "The Ten Commandments" and "Ghostbusters."

Bernstein, Leonard
>BORN: August 25, 1918—Lawrence, MA
>DIED: October 14, 1990—New York

HISTORICAL PERIOD: Modern
COMPOSITIONAL MEDIA: Orchestra, chamber music, ballet, keyboard, choral, opera, musicals, film, TV.
IMPORTANT ITEMS: Popular conductor and composer whose notable works include "Candide" and "West Side Story."

Billings, William
BORN: October 7, 1746—Boston, MA
DIED: September 26, 1800—Boston, MA
HISTORICAL PERIOD: Classical
COMPOSITIONAL MEDIA: Choral.
IMPORTANT ITEMS: Best known for his hymns and anthems.

Bizet, Georges
BORN: October 25, 1838—Paris
DIED: June 3, 1875—Bougival, France
HISTORICAL PERIOD: Romantic
COMPOSITIONAL MEDIA: Opera, orchestra, keyboard, choral, songs.
IMPORTANT ITEMS: Notable works include the opera "Carmen" and the suite "L'Arlésienne."

Bliss, Sir Arthur (Edward Drummond)
BORN: August 2, 1891—London
DIED: March 27, 1975—London
HISTORICAL PERIOD: Modern
COMPOSITIONAL MEDIA: Orchestra, vocal, ballet, chamber music, opera, keyboard, films, TV.
IMPORTANT ITEMS: He was knighted in 1950 and was named Master of the Queens Music in 1953.

Bloch, Ernest
BORN: July 24, 1880—Geneva, Switzerland
DIED: July 15, 1959—Portland, OR
HISTORICAL PERIOD: Modern
COMPOSITIONAL MEDIA: Orchestra, chamber music, keyboard, opera.
IMPORTANT ITEMS: Influential teacher whose pupils included Roger Sessions, Halsey Stevens and Randall Thompson. Many of his works are inspired by Jewish music.

Blow, John
BORN: February 23, 1649—Nottinghamshire, England
DIED: October 1, 1708—Westminster, London
HISTORICAL PERIOD: Baroque
COMPOSITIONAL MEDIA: Keyboard, choral, songs, opera.
IMPORTANT ITEMS: Organist at Westminster Abbey until succeeded by his pupil Purcell.

Boccherini, (Rudolfo) Luigi
BORN: February 19, 1743—Lucca, Italy
DIED: May 28, 1805—Madrid, Spain
HISTORICAL PERIOD: Classical
COMPOSITIONAL MEDIA: Orchestra, chamber music, choral, opera, guitar.
IMPORTANT ITEMS: A professional cellist and composer. Notable works include the minuet from the "String Quintet in E major Op. 13, No. 5."

Bolcom, William (Elden)
BORN: May 26, 1938—Seattle, WA
HISTORICAL PERIOD: Modern
COMPOSITIONAL MEDIA: Orchestra, chamber music, keyboard, opera, electronic.

IMPORTANT ITEMS: Awarded the Pulitzer Prize in 1988 for his "12 Etudes for Piano."

Bolling, Claude
BORN: April 10, 1930—Cannes, France
HISTORICAL PERIOD: Modern
COMPOSITIONAL MEDIA: Chamber music, orchestra, film.
IMPORTANT ITEMS: Jazz pianist and band leader. His compositions blend classical and jazz styles.

Borodin, Alexander (Porfirievich)
BORN: November 12, 1833—St. Petersburg
DIED: February 28, 1887—St. Petersburg
HISTORICAL PERIOD: Romantic
COMPOSITIONAL MEDIA: Orchestra, chamber music, keyboard, opera, songs.
IMPORTANT ITEMS: Notable works include the opera "Prince Igor" and the tone poem "In the Steppes of Central Asia."

Boulanger, Nadia (Juliette)
BORN: September 16, 1887—Paris
DIED: October 22, 1979—Paris
HISTORICAL PERIOD: Modern
COMPOSITIONAL MEDIA: Orchestra, keyboard, choral.
IMPORTANT ITEMS: Important teacher whose pupils included Carter, Copland, Harris, Piston and other well-known American and European composers.

Boulez, Pierre
BORN: March 26, 1925—Montbrison, France
HISTORICAL PERIOD: Modern
COMPOSITIONAL MEDIA: Orchestra, chamber music, keyboard.
IMPORTANT ITEMS: Well respected conductor and leader in developing and promoting serialism and other contemporary music techniques.

Bowie, David
[real name: David Robert Jones]
BORN: January 8, 1947—London
HISTORICAL PERIOD: Modern (Popular)
COMPOSITIONAL MEDIA: Popular songs.
IMPORTANT ITEMS: Notable songs include "Space Oddity" and "Ziggy Stardust."

Boyce, William
BORN: September 11, 1711—London
DIED: February 7, 1779—London
HISTORICAL PERIOD: Baroque
COMPOSITIONAL MEDIA: Vocal, chamber music, orchestra, songs, keyboard, oratorios.
IMPORTANT ITEMS: Named Master of the King's Music in 1759.

Brahms, Johannes
BORN: May 7, 1833—Hamburg, Germany
DIED: April 3, 1897—Vienna
HISTORICAL PERIOD: Romantic
COMPOSITIONAL MEDIA: Orchestra, chamber music, keyboard, choral, songs.
IMPORTANT ITEMS: Notable works include four symphonies, the "Double Concerto" for violin and cello, "Liebeslieder Waltzes" for voices and piano four hands and the "Academic Festival Overture."

Britten, Benjamin
BORN: November 22, 1913—Lowestoft, England
DIED: December 4, 1976—Aldeburgh, England
HISTORICAL PERIOD: Modern
COMPOSITIONAL MEDIA: Orchestra, chamber music, choral, opera, songs, guitar.
IMPORTANT ITEMS: Notable works include "The Young Person's Guide to the Orchestra" and the opera "Peter Grimes."

Brouwer, Leo
BORN: March 1, 1939—Havana
HISTORICAL PERIOD: Modern
COMPOSITIONAL MEDIA: Guitar, keyboard, film, orchestra, chamber music.
IMPORTANT ITEMS: A concert guitarist whose guitar music incorporates Cuban rhythms.

Brown, Earle (Appleton, Jr.)
BORN: December 26, 1926—Lunenburg, MA
HISTORICAL PERIOD: Modern
COMPOSITIONAL MEDIA: Chamber music, keyboard, electronic, orchestra.
IMPORTANT ITEMS: Compositions incorporate aleatoric techniques.

Brubeck, Dave (David Warren)
BORN: December 6, 1920—Concord, CA
HISTORICAL PERIOD: Modern
COMPOSITIONAL MEDIA: Instrumental jazz, orchestra, chamber music, choral, songs.
IMPORTANT ITEMS: Notable works include "Take Five" and "Blue Rondo A La Turk"

Bruch, Max (Karl August)
BORN: January 6, 1838—Cologne, Germany
DIED: October 2, 1920—Friednau, Germany
HISTORICAL PERIOD: Romantic
COMPOSITIONAL MEDIA: Orchestra, chamber music, keyboard, choral, opera, songs.
IMPORTANT ITEMS: Notable works include "Kol Nidrei" for cello and orchestra.

Bruckner, Anton
BORN: September 4, 1824—Ansfelden, Austria
DIED: October 11, 1896—Vienna
HISTORICAL PERIOD: Late Romantic
COMPOSITIONAL MEDIA: Orchestra, chamber music, keyboard, choral.
IMPORTANT ITEMS: Outstanding organist and composer best known for his nine symphonies and "Te Deum" for choir and orchestra.

Bull, John
BORN: c. 1562—Old Radnor, Radnorshire, England
DIED: March 12, 1628—Antwerp
HISTORICAL PERIOD: Late Renaissance
COMPOSITIONAL MEDIA: Keyboard.
IMPORTANT ITEMS: Highly skilled virginalist and organist.

Burgmüller, Johann Friedrich Franz
BORN: December 4, 1806—Regensburg
DIED: February 13, 1874—Beaulieu, France
HISTORICAL PERIOD: Romantic
COMPOSITIONAL MEDIA: Ballet, keyboard, songs.
IMPORTANT ITEMS: Notable works include his piano studies which are standard in pedagogical literature.

Burke, Johnny
    BORN: October 3, 1908—Antioch, CA
    DIED: February 25, 1964—New York
    HISTORICAL PERIOD: Modern (Popular)
    COMPOSITIONAL MEDIA: Popular songs.
    IMPORTANT ITEMS: Notable songs include "What's New," "Pennies from Heaven" and "Misty."

Busoni, Ferruccio (Dante Michelangiolo Benvenuto)
    BORN: April 1, 1866—Empoli, Italy
    DIED: July 27, 1924—Berlin, Germany
    HISTORICAL PERIOD: Late Romantic
    COMPOSITIONAL MEDIA: Keyboard, orchestra, chamber music, opera.
    IMPORTANT ITEMS: A virtuoso pianist who wrote the influential essay "Outline for a New Aesthetics of Music."

Buxtehude, Dietrich
    BORN: 1637—Oldensloe, Holstein
    DIED: May 9, 1707—Lubeck, Germany
    HISTORICAL PERIOD: Baroque
    COMPOSITIONAL MEDIA: Keyboard, chamber music, choral.
    IMPORTANT ITEMS: Virtuoso organist who influenced J.S. Bach.

Byrd, William
    BORN: 1543—Lincolnshire, England
    DIED: July 4, 1623—Stondon, England
    HISTORICAL PERIOD: Renaissance
    COMPOSITIONAL MEDIA: Choral, songs, keyboard, chamber music.
    IMPORTANT ITEMS: Keyboard works are in the Fitzwilliam Virginal Book.

C

Caccini, Giulio
    BORN: October 8, 1551—Tivoli, Italy
    DIED: December 10, 1618—Florence, Italy
    HISTORICAL PERIOD: Renaissance
    COMPOSITIONAL MEDIA: Choral, opera.
    IMPORTANT ITEMS: Notable works include the opera "Euridice."

Cage, John (Milton, Jr.)
    BORN: September 5, 1912—Los Angeles
    DIED: August 12, 1992—New York
    HISTORICAL PERIOD: Modern
    COMPOSITIONAL MEDIA: Orchestra, keyboard, chamber music, choral.
    IMPORTANT ITEMS: Highly experimental composer who, among other techniques, incorporated prepared piano, tape and aleatory techniques.

Caldara, Antonio
    BORN: 1670—Venice
    DIED: December 26, 1736—Vienna
    HISTORICAL PERIOD: Baroque
    COMPOSITIONAL MEDIA: Opera, oratorio, choral, chamber music, songs.
    IMPORTANT ITEMS: Very prolific with over 90 operas, 43 oratorios and 30 masses.

Carissimi, Giacomo
BORN: April 18, 1605—Marino, Italy
DIED: January 12, 1674—Rome
HISTORICAL PERIOD: Baroque
COMPOSITIONAL MEDIA: Choral.
IMPORTANT ITEMS: Best remembered for his development of the oratorio.

Carmichael, Hoagy [Hoagland] (Howard)
BORN: November 22, 1899—Bloomington, IN
DIED: December 27, 1981—Rancho Mirage, CA
HISTORICAL PERIOD: Modern (Popular)
COMPOSITIONAL MEDIA: Popular songs.
IMPORTANT ITEMS: Notable songs include "Stardust" and "Georgia on My Mind."

Carter, Benny
BORN: August 8, 1907—New York
HISTORICAL PERIOD: Modern
COMPOSITIONAL MEDIA: Instrumental jazz, film, TV.
IMPORTANT ITEMS: Notable works include jazz compositions "When Lights Are Low," "Harlem Mood" and the TV score "M Squad."

Carter, Elliott (Cook, Jr.)
BORN: December 11, 1908—New York
HISTORICAL PERIOD: Modern
COMPOSITIONAL MEDIA: Orchestra, chamber music, ballet, keyboard, choral, opera, songs.
IMPORTANT ITEMS: His early works were neo-classical but later turned to serial techniques. Awarded the Pulitzer Prize in 1960 and 1973.

Casadesus, Robert
BORN: April 7, 1899—Paris
DIED: September 19, 1972—Paris
HISTORICAL PERIOD: Modern
COMPOSITIONAL MEDIA: Orchestra, chamber music, keyboard.
IMPORTANT ITEMS: Professional pianist and composer.

Casella, Alfredo
BORN: July 25, 1883—Turin, France
DIED: March 5, 1947—Rome
HISTORICAL PERIOD: Modern
COMPOSITIONAL MEDIA: Orchestra, chamber music, ballet, keyboard, choral, opera.
IMPORTANT ITEMS: Professional pianist, conductor and author. Many compositions are in the neo-classical style.

Cesti, Antonio (Pietro)
BORN: August 5, 1623—Arezzo
DIED: October 14, 1669—Florence
HISTORICAL PERIOD: Baroque
COMPOSITIONAL MEDIA: Operas, vocal, choral.
IMPORTANT ITEMS: One of the most important opera composers of his time.

Chabrier, (Alexis-) Emmanuel
BORN: January 18, 1841—Ambert, Puy de Dome, France
DIED: September 13, 1894—Paris
HISTORICAL PERIOD: Romantic
COMPOSITIONAL MEDIA: Orchestra, opera, keyboard, songs.

IMPORTANT ITEMS: Notable works include "España" for orchestra.

Chaminade, Cecile (Louise Stéphanie)
BORN: August 8, 1857—Paris, France
DIED: April 13, 1944—Monte Carlo, France
HISTORICAL PERIOD: Romantic
COMPOSITIONAL MEDIA: Keyboard, orchestra, chamber music, choral, songs.
IMPORTANT ITEMS: Successful concert pianist.

Chausson, (Amédée) Ernest
BORN: January 20, 1855—Paris
DIED: June 10, 1899—Limay, France
HISTORICAL PERIOD: Romantic
COMPOSITIONAL MEDIA: Opera, vocal, orchestra, chamber music, songs.
IMPORTANT ITEMS: Highly influenced by the music of Wagner and Franck.

Chavez (y Ramirez), Carlos (Antonio de Padua)
BORN: June 13, 1899—Mexico City
DIED: August 2, 1978—Mexico City
HISTORICAL PERIOD: Modern
COMPOSITIONAL MEDIA: Symphony, keyboard, ballet, choral, vocal, chamber music.
IMPORTANT ITEMS: He founded and conducted Mexico's first symphony orchestra.

Cherubini, Luigi (Carlo Zenobio Saluatore Maria)
BORN: September 14, 1760—Florence
DIED: March 13, 1842—Paris
HISTORICAL PERIOD: Classical
COMPOSITIONAL MEDIA: Orchestra, chamber music, ballet, keyboard, choral, opera.
IMPORTANT ITEMS: His music inspired Beethoven. Notable works include his "Requiem No. 2" in D minor.

Childs, Barney
BORN: February 13, 1926—Spokane, WA
HISTORICAL PERIOD: Modern
COMPOSITIONAL MEDIA: Orchestra, chamber music, choral.
IMPORTANT ITEMS: Compositions include aleatory techniques.

Chopin, Frédéric (-François)
BORN: February 22, 1810—Zelazowa Wola, Poland
DIED: October 17, 1849—Paris
HISTORICAL PERIOD: Romantic
COMPOSITIONAL MEDIA: Keyboard, orchestra, chamber music, songs.
IMPORTANT ITEMS: A professional pianist whose notable works include mazurkas, waltzes, polonaises and numerous other piano compositions.

Chou, Wen-chung
BORN: June 29, 1923—Chefoo, China
HISTORICAL PERIOD: Modern
COMPOSITIONAL MEDIA: Orchestra, band, chamber music, keyboard, film.
IMPORTANT ITEMS: Incorporated the principles of I Ching in some compositions.

Cimarosa, Domenico
BORN: December 17, 1749—Aversa, Italy
DIED: January 11, 1801—Venice

HISTORICAL PERIOD: Classical
COMPOSITIONAL MEDIA: Opera, chamber music, keyboard, choral, songs.
IMPORTANT ITEMS: Prolific composer of Italian opera buffa.

Clarke, Jeremiah
BORN: 1673—London
DIED: December 1, 1707—London
HISTORICAL PERIOD: Baroque
COMPOSITIONAL MEDIA: Keyboard, choral, opera, songs, theatrical.
IMPORTANT ITEMS: Notable works include the "Trumpet Voluntary."

Clementi, Muzio
BORN: January 23, 1752—Rome
DIED: March 10, 1832—Evesham, England
HISTORICAL PERIOD: Classical
COMPOSITIONAL MEDIA: Orchestra, keyboard.
IMPORTANT ITEMS: Professional pianist and conductor. Notable works include his collection of piano studies "Gradus ad Parnassum."

Cohan, Geroge M.
BORN: July 3, 1878—Providence, RI
DIED: November 5, 1942—New York
HISTORICAL PERIOD: Modern (Popular)
COMPOSITIONAL MEDIA: Popular songs.
IMPORTANT ITEMS: Notable songs include "Over There" and "Yankee Doodle Dandy."

Coleman, Cy
[real name: Seymour Kaufman]
BORN: June 14, 1929—New York
HISTORICAL PERIOD: Modern (Popular)
COMPOSITIONAL MEDIA: Popular songs, musicals, radio, TV.
IMPORTANT ITEMS: Notable works include scores to the Broadway musicals "Barnum," "Sweet Charity" and the song "Hey Look Me Over."

Coleridge-Taylor, Samuel
BORN: August 15, 1875—London
DIED: September 1, 1912—Croydon, England
HISTORICAL PERIOD: Romantic
COMPOSITIONAL MEDIA: Orchestra, chamber music, opera, vocal, keyboard.
IMPORTANT ITEMS: Most notable work is his "Song of Hiawatha" trilogy.

Coleman, Ornette
BORN: March 9, 1930—Fort Worth, TX
HISTORICAL PERIOD: Modern
COMPOSITIONAL MEDIA: Instrumental jazz, chamber music, orchestra.
IMPORTANT ITEMS: Influential jazz saxophonist and composer. Notable works include "Lonely Woman."

Copland, Aaron
BORN: November 14, 1900—Brooklyn, NY
DIED: December 2, 1990—Westchester, NY
HISTORICAL PERIOD: Modern
COMPOSITIONAL MEDIA: Orchestra, chamber music, ballet, keyboard, choral, songs, opera, film.
IMPORTANT ITEMS: Very popular American composer who incorporated American folk music, jazz, and serial techniques in his music. Notable works include "Lincoln Portrait," "Rodeo," "Appalachian

Spring" and "Fanfare for the Common Man."

Corelli, Arcangelo
    BORN: February 17, 1653—Fusignano, Italy
    DIED: January 8, 1713—Rome
    HISTORICAL PERIOD: Baroque
    COMPOSITIONAL MEDIA: Orchestra, chamber music.
    IMPORTANT ITEMS: Famous virtuoso violinist and composer who created the concerto grosso.

Corigliano, John (Paul)
    BORN: February 16, 1938—New York
    HISTORICAL PERIOD: Modern
    COMPOSITIONAL MEDIA: Orchestra, chamber music, choral, electronic, theatrical.
    IMPORTANT ITEMS: Notable works include the opera "The Ghosts of Versailles" and his symphony No. 1.

Costello, Elvis
    [real name: Declan McManus]
    BORN: August 25, 1954—London
    HISTORICAL PERIOD: Modern (Popular)
    COMPOSITIONAL MEDIA: Popular songs.
    IMPORTANT ITEMS: Popular singer and songwriter. Notable songs include "Watching the Detectives."

Couperin, François
    BORN: November 10, 1668—Paris
    DIED: September 11, 1733—Paris
    HISTORICAL PERIOD: Baroque
    COMPOSITIONAL MEDIA: Choral, chamber music, keyboard.
    IMPORTANT ITEMS: Notable works include his book on harpsichord playing, "L'art de toucher la clavecin" which is a standard of pedagogical literature

Cowell, Henry (Dixon)
    BORN: March 11, 1897—Menlo Park, CA
    DIED: December 1910, 1965—Shady, NY
    HISTORICAL PERIOD: Modern
    COMPOSITIONAL MEDIA: Orchestra, chamber music, ballet, keyboard, choral, opera, songs.
    IMPORTANT ITEMS: Innovative composer whose compositions incorporate tone clusters, playing on the inside of the piano and aleatory techniques.

Cramer, Johann Baptist
    BORN: February 24, 1771— Mannheim
    DIED: April 16, 1858—London
    HISTORICAL PERIOD: Classical
    COMPOSITIONAL MEDIA: Keyboard, chamber music, orchestra.
    IMPORTANT ITEMS: Best known for his piano method.

Creston, Paul
    [real name: Giuseppe Guttoveggio]
    BORN: October 10, 1906—New York
    DIED: August 24, 1985—San Diego, CA
    HISTORICAL PERIOD: Modern
    COMPOSITIONAL MEDIA: Orchestra, chamber music, keyboard, choral.
    IMPORTANT ITEMS: Prolific composer and author.

Crüger, Johann
    BORN April 9, 1598—Gross Breese, Prussia
    DIED: February 23, 1662—Berlin
    HISTORICAL PERIOD: Baroque
    COMPOSITIONAL MEDIA: Choral, orchestra.

IMPORTANT ITEMS: Notable works include the chorale melodies "Nun danket alle Gott" and "Jesu meine Freude" which were later used by Bach.

Crumb, George (Henry)
BORN: October 24, 1929—Charleston, WV
HISTORICAL PERIOD: Modern
COMPOSITIONAL MEDIA: Orchestra, chamber music, keyboard, choral, songs, electronic.
IMPORTANT ITEMS: Awarded the Pulitzer Prize in 1968 for "Echoes of Time and the River." Notable works include "Ancient Voices of Children."

Cui, César (Antonovich)
BORN: January 18, 1835—Vilna, Russia
DIED: March 26, 1918—Petrograd, Russia
HISTORICAL PERIOD: Romantic
COMPOSITIONAL MEDIA: Orchestra, chamber music, keyboard, choral, opera, songs.
IMPORTANT ITEMS: A member of the Russian Five.

Czerny, Carl
BORN: February 20, 1791—Vienna
DIED: July 15, 1857—Vienna
HISTORICAL PERIOD: Classical
COMPOSITIONAL MEDIA: Orchestra, chamber music, keyboard, choral.
IMPORTANT ITEMS: Notable works include keyboard exercises which are a standard in pedagogical literature.

D

Dahl, Ingolf
BORN: June 9, 1912—Hamburg, Germany
DIED: August 6, 1970—Frutigen, Switzerland
HISTORICAL PERIOD: Modern
COMPOSITIONAL MEDIA: Orchestra, chamber music, keyboard, choral.
IMPORTANT ITEMS: Teacher at the University of Southern California.

Dalcroze, Emile Jaques
BORN: July 6, 1865—Vienna
DIED: July 1, 1950—Geneva, Switzerland
HISTORICAL PERIOD: Late Romantic
COMPOSITIONAL MEDIA: Orchestra, chamber music, keyboard, choral, opera, songs, theatrical.
IMPORTANT ITEMS: Developed eurhythmics.

Dallapiccola, Luigi
BORN: February 3, 1904—Pisino, Italy
DIED: February 19, 1975—Florence, Italy
HISTORICAL PERIOD: Modern
COMPOSITIONAL MEDIA: Orchestra, chamber music, keyboard, choral, opera, songs.
IMPORTANT ITEMS: Compositions incorporate twelve-tone techniques.

Damrosch, Walter Johannes
BORN: January 30, 1862—Breslau, Germany
DIED: December 22, 1950—New York
HISTORICAL PERIOD: Late Romantic
COMPOSITIONAL MEDIA: Choral, opera, songs.
IMPORTANT ITEMS: Conductor who premiered many famous works in the United States.

Davidovsky, Mario
>BORN: March 4, 1934—Buenos Aires, Argentina
>HISTORICAL PERIOD: Modern
>COMPOSITIONAL MEDIA: Orchestra, chamber music, keyboard, electronic.
>IMPORTANT ITEMS: Awarded the Pulitzer Prize in 1971 for "Synchronisms No. 6" for piano and electronics.

Davies, Peter Maxwell
>BORN: September 8, 1934—Manchester, England
>HISTORICAL PERIOD: Modern
>COMPOSITIONAL MEDIA: Orchestra, chamber music, keyboard, choral, opera, electronic.
>IMPORTANT ITEMS: Notable works include "Eight Songs for a Mad King."

Davis, Miles (Dewy, III)
>BORN: May 25, 1926—Alton, IL
>DIED: September 28, 1991—Santa Monica, CA
>HISTORICAL PERIOD: Modern (Jazz)
>COMPOSITIONAL MEDIA: Popular instrumental.
>IMPORTANT ITEMS: Influential jazz trumpeter who blended rock rhythms and jazz in his compositions.

Debussy, (Achille-) Claude
>BORN: August 22, 1862—Saint Germain-en-Laye, France
>DIED: March 25, 1918—Paris
>HISTORICAL PERIOD: Modern
>COMPOSITIONAL MEDIA: Orchestra, chamber music, ballet, keyboard, choral, opera, songs.
>IMPORTANT ITEMS: Important impressionist composer. Notable works include "La Mer" for orchestra, the opera "Pelléas et Mélisande" and numerous pieces for piano.

Delibes, (Clément Philibert) Léo
>BORN: February 21, 1836—St. Germain-du-Val, France
>DIED: January 16, 1891—Paris
>HISTORICAL PERIOD: Romantic
>COMPOSITIONAL MEDIA: Ballet, choral, opera, songs.
>IMPORTANT ITEMS: Successful composer of operas and ballets.

Delius, (Fritz) Frederick
>BORN: January 29, 1862—Bradford, England
>DIED: June 10, 1934—Grez-sur-Loing, France
>HISTORICAL PERIOD: Late Romantic
>COMPOSITIONAL MEDIA: Orchestra, chamber music, choral, opera, songs.
>IMPORTANT ITEMS: Compositions include romantic and impressionist elements.

Dello Joio, Norman
>BORN: January 24, 1913—New York
>HISTORICAL PERIOD: Modern
>COMPOSITIONAL MEDIA: Orchestra, chamber music, keyboard, choral, opera, band.
>IMPORTANT ITEMS: Notable works include the opera "The Triumph of St. Joan."

Del Tredici, David (Walter)
>BORN: March 16, 1937—Cloverdale, CA
>HISTORICAL PERIOD: Modern

COMPOSITIONAL MEDIA: Orchestra, chamber music, keyboard, choral, songs.
IMPORTANT ITEMS: Most famous compositions are based on "Alice in Wonderland" by Lewis Carroll.

des Prez, Josquin
BORN: c. 1440—Beauvoir, France
DIED: August 27, 1521—Conde-sur-l'Escaut, France
HISTORICAL PERIOD: Renaissance
COMPOSITIONAL MEDIA: Choral, chamber music.
IMPORTANT ITEMS: Influential Renaissance composer of expressive choral music.

Diabelli, Anton
BORN: September 5, 1781—Mattsee, Germany
DIED: April 8, 1858—Vienna
HISTORICAL PERIOD: Classical
COMPOSITIONAL MEDIA: Chamber music, ballet, keyboard, choral, opera, songs.
IMPORTANT ITEMS: Beethoven based his "Diabelli Variations" on a waltz theme by Diabelli.

Diamond, David (Leo)
BORN: July 9, 1915—Rochester, NY
HISTORICAL PERIOD: Modern
COMPOSITIONAL MEDIA: Orchestra, chamber music, ballet, keyboard, choral, songs.
IMPORTANT ITEMS: Composer of highly contrapuntal music who adopted serial techniques in the 1950s.

Diamond, Neil (Leslie)
BORN: January 24, 1941—New York
HISTORICAL PERIOD: Modern (Popular)
COMPOSITIONAL MEDIA: Popular songs, film.
IMPORTANT ITEMS: Notable songs include "Sweet Caroline."

d'Indy, Vincent: See Indy, Vincent d'

Dittersdorf, Karl Ditters von
BORN: November 2, 1739—Vienna
DIED: October 24, 1799—Castle Rothlhotta, Bohemia
HISTORICAL PERIOD: Classical
COMPOSITIONAL MEDIA: Orchestra, chamber music, ballet, keyboard, choral, opera.
IMPORTANT ITEMS: An important member of the classical Viennese school.

Dohnanyi, Ernö (Ernst von)
BORN: July 27, 1877—Pressburg, Bratislava
DIED: February 9, 1960—New York
HISTORICAL PERIOD: Late Romantic/Modern
COMPOSITIONAL MEDIA: Orchestra, keyboard, chamber music, vocal, opera.
IMPORTANT ITEMS: His most famous work is "Variations on a Nursery Song" for piano and orchestra.

Donaldson, Walter
BORN: February 15, 1893—New York
DIED: July 15, 1947—New York
HISTORICAL PERIOD: Modern (Popular)
COMPOSITIONAL MEDIA: Popular songs.
IMPORTANT ITEMS: Notable songs include "My Mammy," "Yes Sir, That's My Baby" and "Makin' Whoopee."

Donizetti, Gaetano
BORN: November 29, 1797—Bergamo, Italy
DIED: April 1, 1848—Bergamo, Italy
HISTORICAL PERIOD: Romantic
COMPOSITIONAL MEDIA: Opera, chamber music, keyboard, choral.
IMPORTANT ITEMS: Notable works include the operas "Lucia di Lamermoor" and "Don Pasquale."

Dowland, John
BORN: December 1562—near Dublin, England
DIED: January 21, 1626—London
HISTORICAL PERIOD: Renaissance
COMPOSITIONAL MEDIA: Songs, lute, chamber music.
IMPORTANT ITEMS: Virtuoso lutenist and singer whose works were harmonically advanced for their time.

Druckman, Jacob (Raphael)
BORN: June 6, 1928—Philadelphia, PA
HISTORICAL PERIOD: Modern
COMPOSITIONAL MEDIA: Orchestra, chamber music, choral, electronic.
IMPORTANT ITEMS: Awarded the Pulitzer Prize in 1972 for his orchestral work "Windows."

Dufay, Guillaume
BORN: c. 1400—Cambrai, France
DIED: November 27, 1474—Cambrai, France
HISTORICAL PERIOD: Late Medieval/Early Renaissance
COMPOSITIONAL MEDIA: Choral.
IMPORTANT ITEMS: Most famous for his cantus firmus Masses, motets and chansons.

Dukas, Paul
BORN: October 1, 1865—Paris
DIED: May 17, 1935—Paris
HISTORICAL PERIOD: Late Romantic
COMPOSITIONAL MEDIA: Orchestra, chamber music, keyboard, opera, ballet.
IMPORTANT ITEMS: Notable works include "L'Apprenti Sorcier" (The Sorcerer's Apprentice).

Duke, Vernon
[real name: Vladimir Dukelsky]
BORN: October 10, 1903—Parfianovka, Russia
DIED: January 16, 1969—Santa Monica, CA
HISTORICAL PERIOD: Modern
COMPOSITIONAL MEDIA: Orchestra, chamber music, ballet, keyboard, choral, popular songs.
IMPORTANT ITEMS: Notable popular songs include "April in Paris."

Dunstable, John
BORN: c. 1390—Dunstable, England
DIED: December 24, 1453—London
HISTORICAL PERIOD: Medieval
COMPOSITIONAL MEDIA: Choral.
IMPORTANT ITEMS: Influential composer of Masses and isorhythmic motets.

Dupre, Marcel
BORN: May 3, 1886—Rouen, France
DIED: May 30, 1971—Meudon, France
HISTORICAL PERIOD: Modern

COMPOSITIONAL MEDIA: Organ, choral.
IMPORTANT ITEMS: Award winning composer and organist.

Dussek, Jan (Johann) Ladislav
BORN: February 12, 1760—Caslav, Bohemia
DIED: March 20, 1812—St Germain-en-Laye
HISTORICAL PERIOD: Classical
COMPOSITIONAL MEDIA: Keyboard, chamber music, orchestra, choral.
IMPORTANT ITEMS: Notable works include many influential pieces for piano.

Dvořák, Antonin (Leopold)
BORN: September 8, 1841—Muhlhausen, Bohemia
DIED: May 1, 1904—Prague, Czechoslovakia
HISTORICAL PERIOD: Romantic
COMPOSITIONAL MEDIA: Orchestra, chamber music, keyboard, choral, opera, songs.
IMPORTANT ITEMS: Notable works include the symphony in E minor "From the New World."

Dylan, Bob
[real name: Robert Allen Zimmerman]
BORN: May 24, 1941—Duluth, MN
HISTORICAL PERIOD: Modern (Popular)
COMPOSITIONAL MEDIA: Popular songs.
IMPORTANT ITEMS: Notable songs include "Blowin' in the Wind," "The Times They Are A-Changin'" and "Mr. Tambourine Man."

E

Elgar, Sir Edward (William)
BORN: June 2, 1857—Broadheath, England
DIED: February 23, 1934—Worcester, England
HISTORICAL PERIOD: Late Romantic
COMPOSITIONAL MEDIA: Orchestra, chamber music, opera, choral, songs, keyboard.
IMPORTANT ITEMS: Notable works include "Enigma Variations" and his "Pomp and Circumstance" marches.

Ellington, "Duke" (Edward Kennedy)
BORN: April 29, 1899—Washington, DC
DIED: May 24, 1974—New York
HISTORICAL PERIOD: Modern (Popular)
COMPOSITIONAL MEDIA: Instrumental jazz, orchestra, chamber music, choral, popular songs.
IMPORTANT ITEMS: One of the most influential jazz composers of the 20th century. Notable songs include "Satin Doll," "Sophisticated Lady," "Take the A Train" and "Harlem Air Shaft."

Enesco [Enescu], Georges
BORN: August 19, 1881—Liveni-Virnav, Romania
DIED: May 4, 1955—Paris
HISTORICAL PERIOD: Modern
COMPOSITIONAL MEDIA: Orchestra, chamber music, keyboard, choral, opera.
IMPORTANT ITEMS: Many of his compositions incorporate Romanian folk idioms.

Erb, Donald (James)
BORN: January 17, 1927—Youngstown, OH
HISTORICAL PERIOD: Modern

COMPOSITIONAL MEDIA: Orchestra, chamber music, keyboard, choral, electronic, band.
IMPORTANT ITEMS: Incorporates many different styles into his compositions including jazz, serial and aleatory techniques.

F

Falla (y Matheu), Manuel (Maria) de

BORN: November 23, 1876—Cadiz, Spain
DIED: November 14, 1946—Alta Gracia, Argentina
HISTORICAL PERIOD: Modern
COMPOSITIONAL MEDIA: Orchestra, chamber music, ballet, keyboard, opera, songs.
IMPORTANT ITEMS: Notable works include the ballets "El amor brujo" and "The Three-Cornered Hat."

Fauré, Gabriel (Urbain)

BORN: May 12, 1845—Pamiers, France
DIED: November 4, 1924—Paris
HISTORICAL PERIOD: Late Romantic
COMPOSITIONAL MEDIA: Chamber music, orchestra, keyboard, choral, opera, songs.
IMPORTANT ITEMS: Important composer who used old modes, counterpoint and free dissonance. Notable works include his "Requiem."

Feldman, Morton

BORN: January 12, 1926—New York
DIED: September 3, 1987—Buffalo, NY
HISTORICAL PERIOD: Modern
COMPOSITIONAL MEDIA: Orchestra, chamber music, choral, electronic.
IMPORTANT ITEMS: Compositions incorporate graphic notation and indeterminancy.

Field, John

BORN: July 26, 1782—Dublin
DIED: January 23, 1837—Moscow
HISTORICAL PERIOD: Romantic
COMPOSITIONAL MEDIA: Keyboard, chamber music, orchestra.
IMPORTANT ITEMS: The originator of the keyboard "Nocturne."

Fillmore, (James) Henry (Jr.)

BORN: December 2, 1881—Cincinnati, OH
DIED: December 7, 1956—Miami, FL
HISTORICAL PERIOD: Modern
COMPOSITIONAL MEDIA: Band, songs.
IMPORTANT ITEMS: Notable works include the marches "American We" and "His Honor."

Finney, Ross Lee

BORN: December 23, 1906—Wells, MN
HISTORICAL PERIOD: Modern
COMPOSITIONAL MEDIA: Orchestra, chamber music, keyboard, choral, songs, electronic.
IMPORTANT ITEMS: Compositions incorporate serial techniques. Studied with Alban Berg.

Flowtow, Friedrich (Adolf Ferdinand) von
BORN: April 27, 1813—Teutendorf, Germany
DIED: January 24, 1883—Darmstadt, Germany
HISTORICAL PERIOD: Romantic
COMPOSITIONAL MEDIA: Opera, ballet, orchestra, chamber music, songs.
IMPORTANT ITEMS: Notable operas include "Martha" and "Alessandro Stradella."

Foss, Lukas [real name: Lukas Fuchs]
BORN: August 15, 1922—Berlin, Germany
HISTORICAL PERIOD: Modern
COMPOSITIONAL MEDIA: Orchestra, chamber music, ballet, keyboard, choral, opera, electronic.
IMPORTANT ITEMS: Compositions include a variety of styles including American folk music and serial techniques.

Foster, Stephen Collins
BORN: July 4, 1826—Lawrenceville, PA
DIED: January 13, 1864—New York
HISTORICAL PERIOD: Romantic
COMPOSITIONAL MEDIA: Songs.
IMPORTANT ITEMS: Notable songs include "Old Folks at Home," "Oh, Susanna!" and "Camptown Races."

Françaix, Jean
BORN: May 23, 1912—Le Mans, France
HISTORICAL PERIOD: Modern
COMPOSITIONAL MEDIA: Orchestra, chamber music, keyboard, choral, songs, ballet, opera, film.
IMPORTANT ITEMS: Prolific composer and pianist.

Franck, César (-August-Jean-Guillaume-Hubert)
BORN: December 10, 1822—Liege, Belgium
DIED: November 8, 1890 Paris
HISTORICAL PERIOD: Romantic
COMPOSITIONAL MEDIA: Orchestra, chamber music, keyboard, choral, opera, songs.
IMPORTANT ITEMS: Notable works include his symphony in D minor.

Frescobaldi, Girolamo
BORN: September 9, 1583—Ferrara, Italy
DIED: March 1, 1643—Rome
HISTORICAL PERIOD: Baroque
COMPOSITIONAL MEDIA: Keyboard, chamber music, choral.
IMPORTANT ITEMS: The most famous organist of his time and a significant composer of keyboard music.

Friml, (Charles) Rudolf
BORN: December 2, 1879—Prague, Czechoslovakia
DIED: November 12, 1972—Hollywood, CA
HISTORICAL PERIOD: Modern (Popular)
COMPOSITIONAL MEDIA: Operetta, film.
IMPORTANT ITEMS: Notable works include the operettas "Rose Marie," "The Firefly" and the "Vagabond King."

Fux, Johann Joseph
BORN: 1660—Hirtenfeld, near St. Marein, Styria
DIED: February 13, 1741—Vienna
HISTORICAL PERIOD: Baroque
COMPOSITIONAL MEDIA: Opera, oratorio, choral, keyboard.
IMPORTANT ITEMS: Notable works include his treatise on counterpoint, "Gradus ad Parnassum."

G

Gabrieli, Andrea
> BORN: c. 1510—Venice
> DIED: 1586—Venice
> HISTORICAL PERIOD: Renaissance
> COMPOSITIONAL MEDIA: Choral, chamber music, keyboard.
> IMPORTANT ITEMS: Versatile composer who taught his nephew Giovanni Gabrieli.

Gabrieli, Giovanni
> BORN: 1554-1557—Venice
> DIED: August 12, 1612—Venice
> HISTORICAL PERIOD: Renaissance
> COMPOSITIONAL MEDIA: Choral, chamber music, organ.
> IMPORTANT ITEMS: Best known for antiphonal choral works.

Gade, Niels (Wilhelm)
> BORN: February 22, 1817—Copenhagen
> DIED: December 21, 1890—Copenhagen
> HISTORICAL PERIOD: Romantic
> COMPOSITIONAL MEDIA: Orchestra, chamber music, keyboard, choral, opera, songs, ballet.
> IMPORTANT ITEMS: Prolific Danish composer influenced by the works of Mendelssohn and Schumann.

Gershwin, George
> BORN: September 26, 1898—Brooklyn, NY
> DIED: July 11, 1937—Beverly Hills, CA
> HISTORICAL PERIOD: Modern
> COMPOSITIONAL MEDIA: Orchestra, keyboard, musicals, popular songs, film.
> IMPORTANT ITEMS: Compositions combined elements of classical and jazz. Notable works include "An American in Paris," "Rhapsody in Blue" and the opera "Porgy and Bess."

Gesualdo, Don Carlo, Prince of Venosa
> BORN: c. 1560—Naples
> DIED: September 8, 1613
> HISTORICAL PERIOD: Renaissance
> COMPOSITIONAL MEDIA: Choral, songs.
> IMPORTANT ITEMS: Best known for his highly chromatic madrigals.

Giannini, Vittorio
> BORN: October 19, 1903—Philadelphia, PA
> DIED: November 28, 1966—New York
> HISTORICAL PERIOD: Modern
> COMPOSITIONAL MEDIA: Orchestra, chamber music, band, keyboard, choral, opera, songs.
> IMPORTANT ITEMS: Prolific composer and teacher.

Gibbons, Orlando
> BORN: December 25, 1583—Oxford, England
> DIED: June 5, 1625—Canterbury, England
> HISTORICAL PERIOD: Renaissance
> COMPOSITIONAL MEDIA: Choral, chamber music.
> IMPORTANT ITEMS: A master of the polyphonic style and great organist.

Ginastera, Alberto (Evaristo)
BORN: April 11, 1916—Buenos Aires, Argentina
DIED: June 25, 1983—Geneva
HISTORICAL PERIOD: Modern
COMPOSITIONAL MEDIA: Orchestra, chamber music, ballet, keyboard, choral, songs, guitar.
IMPORTANT ITEMS: Compositions incorporate serial, aleatoric and micro tonal techniques.

Glass, Philip
BORN: January 31, 1937—Baltimore
HISTORICAL PERIOD: Modern
COMPOSITIONAL MEDIA: Chamber music, opera, ballet, film, orchestra.
IMPORTANT ITEMS: Compositions are in the minimalist style.

Glazunov, Alexander (Konstantinovich)
BORN: August 10, 1865—St. Petersburg, Russia
DIED: March 21, 1936—Paris
HISTORICAL PERIOD: Romantic
COMPOSITIONAL MEDIA: Orchestra, chamber music, ballet, keyboard, choral, songs.
IMPORTANT ITEMS: Prolific composer and teacher. Notable works include nine symphonies and the ballet "Raymonda."

Gliere, Reinhold (Moritzovich)
BORN: January 11, 1875—Kiev, Russia
DIED: June 23, 1956—Moscow
HISTORICAL PERIOD: Late Romantic
COMPOSITIONAL MEDIA: Orchestra, chamber music, ballet, keyboard, opera, songs.
IMPORTANT ITEMS: Notable works include Symphony No. 3 "Ilya Muromets."

Glinka, Mikhail (Ivanovich)
BORN: June 1, 1804—Novosspaskoye, Russia
DIED: February 15, 1857—Berlin
HISTORICAL PERIOD: Romantic
COMPOSITIONAL MEDIA: Orchestra, chamber music, ballet, keyboard, choral, opera, songs.
IMPORTANT ITEMS: Sometimes called the "Father of Russian Music." Notoble works include the opera "Russlan and Ludmilla."

Gluck, Christoph Willibald (von)
BORN: July 2, 1714—Erasbach, Austria
DIED: November 15, 1787—Vienna
HISTORICAL PERIOD: Classical
COMPOSITIONAL MEDIA: Orchestra, chamber music, ballet, choral, opera, songs.
IMPORTANT ITEMS: Highly influential composer of opera including "Orfeo ed Erudice."

Gold, Ernest
BORN: July 13, 1921—Vienna
HISTORICAL PERIOD: Modern
COMPOSITIONAL MEDIA: Orchestra, chamber music, keyboard, film.
IMPORTANT ITEMS: Notable works include the film score for "Exodus."

Gossec, François Joseph
BORN: January 17, 1734—Vergnies, Belgium
DIED: February 16, 1829—Paris
HISTORICAL PERIOD: Classical
COMPOSITIONAL MEDIA: Orchestra, chamber music, ballet, choral, opera.

IMPORTANT ITEMS: Innovator of orchestration. Wrote a considerable amount of choral music for the French revolution.

Gottschalk, Louis Moreau
BORN: May 8, 1829—New Orleans, LA
DIED: December 18, 1869—Rio de Janeiro, Brazil
HISTORICAL PERIOD: Romantic
COMPOSITIONAL MEDIA: Orchestra, piano, opera, songs.
IMPORTANT ITEMS: Virtuoso pianist, most famous for his piano compositions.

Gould, Morton
BORN: December 10, 1913—Richmond Hill NY
DIED: February 21, 1996—Orlando, FL
HISTORICAL PERIOD: Modern
COMPOSITIONAL MEDIA: Orchestra, chamber music, ballet, keyboard, choral, film, TV, band.
IMPORTANT ITEMS: Many of his pieces have American themes. Awarded the Pulitzer Prize in 1995 for "String Music."

Gounod, Charles (François)
BORN: June 17, 1818—Paris
DIED: October 18, 1893—Paris
HISTORICAL PERIOD: Romantic
COMPOSITIONAL MEDIA: Opera, orchestra, chamber music, keyboard, choral, songs.
IMPORTANT ITEMS: Notable works include the opera "Faust."

Grainger, (George) Percy (Aldridge)
BORN: July 8, 1882—Melbourne, Australia
DIED: February 20, 1961—White Plains, NY
HISTORICAL PERIOD: Modern
COMPOSITIONAL MEDIA: Orchestra, chamber music, keyboard, choral, songs, band, electronic.
IMPORTANT ITEMS: A collector of British folk songs. Notable works include "Shepherd's Hey" and "Lincolnshire Posy."

Granados (y Campiña), Enrique
BORN: July 27, 1867—Lerida, Spain
DIED: March 24, 1916—At sea
HISTORICAL PERIOD: Romantic
COMPOSITIONAL MEDIA: Opera, orchestra, vocal, chamber music, keyboard.
IMPORTANT ITEMS: Notable works include "Goyescas."

Green, Johnny
[real name: John Waldo Green]
BORN: October 10, 1908—New York
DIED: May 15, 1989—Beverly Hills, CA
HISTORICAL PERIOD: Modern (Popular)
COMPOSITIONAL MEDIA: Popular songs, film.
IMPORTANT ITEMS: Notable songs include "Body and Soul" and "I Cover the Waterfront."

Grieg, Edvard (Hagerup)
BORN: June 15, 1843—Bergen, Norway
DIED: September 4, 1907—Bergen, Norway
HISTORICAL PERIOD: Romantic
COMPOSITIONAL MEDIA: Orchestra, chamber music, keyboard, choral, songs.
IMPORTANT ITEMS: Best known for incidental music to Ibsen's "Peer Gynt" and his piano concerto.

Griffes, Charles Tomlinson
> BORN: September 17, 1884—Elmira, NY
> DIED: April 8, 1920—New York
> HISTORICAL PERIOD: Modern
> COMPOSITIONAL MEDIA: Orchestra, chamber music, keyboard, choral, songs, theatrical.
> IMPORTANT ITEMS: Considered the foremost American impressionist.

Grofé, Ferde [Ferdinand Rudolph van]
> BORN: March 27, 1892—New York
> DIED: April 3, 1972—Santa Monica, CA
> HISTORICAL PERIOD: Modern
> COMPOSITIONAL MEDIA: Orchestra, keyboard.
> IMPORTANT ITEMS: Pianist and arranger for Paul Whiteman's band who scored Gershwin's "Rhapsody in Blue." Notable works include the orchestral composition "Grand Canyon Suite."

Guilmant, Felix Alexandre
> BORN: March 12, 1837—Boulogne, France
> DIED: March 29, 1911—Meudon, France
> HISTORICAL PERIOD: Romantic
> COMPOSITIONAL MEDIA: Orchestra, keyboard, choral.
> IMPORTANT ITEMS: Virtuoso organist, composer and teacher.

Guthrie, Woody [Woodrow] (Wilson)
> BORN: July 14, 1912—Okemah, OK
> DIED: October 3, 1967—New York
> HISTORICAL PERIOD: Modern (Popular)
> COMPOSITIONAL MEDIA: Popular songs.
> IMPORTANT ITEMS: Notable songs include "This Land is Your Land."

H

Hamlisch, Marvin (Frederic)
> BORN: June 2, 1944—New York
> HISTORICAL PERIOD: Modern (Popular)
> COMPOSITIONAL MEDIA: Musicals, film.
> IMPORTANT ITEMS: Notable musicals include "A Chorus Line."

Handel, George Frideric
> BORN: February 23, 1685—Halle
> DIED: April 14, 1759—London
> HISTORICAL PERIOD: Baroque
> COMPOSITIONAL MEDIA: Choral, opera, orchestra, chamber music, keyboard, songs.
> IMPORTANT ITEMS: One of the most important baroque composers. Notable works include his oratorios "Messiah" and "Judas Maccabeus" and the orchestral compositions "Water Music" and "Royal Fireworks Music."

Handy, W.C. [William Christopher]
> BORN: November 16, 1873—Florence, AL
> DIED: March 28, 1958—New York
> HISTORICAL PERIOD: Modern (Popular)
> COMPOSITIONAL MEDIA: Popular songs.
> IMPORTANT ITEMS: Known as "the father of the blues." Notable songs include "St. Louis Blues."

Hanon, Charles-Louis
BORN: July 2, 1819—Renescure, France
DIED: March 19, 1900—Boulogne-sur-Mer, France
HISTORICAL PERIOD: Romantic
COMPOSITIONAL MEDIA: Keyboard.
IMPORTANT ITEMS: Notable works include "60 Progressive Studies for Piano."

Hanson, Howard (Harold)
BORN: October 28, 1896—Wahoo, NE
DIED: February 26, 1981—Rochester, NY
HISTORICAL PERIOD: Modern
COMPOSITIONAL MEDIA: Orchestra, chamber music, ballet, keyboard, choral, opera, songs.
IMPORTANT ITEMS: Awarded Pulizter Prize in 1944 for "The Requiem." Notable works include the opera "Merry Mount."

Harbison, John (Harris)
BORN: December 20, 1938—Orange, NJ
HISTORICAL PERIOD: Modern
COMPOSITIONAL MEDIA: Orchestra, chamber music, choral, opera, ballet.
IMPORTANT ITEMS: Awarded the Pulitzer Prize in 1987 for his vocal work "The Flight Into Egypt."

Harris, Roy (Leroy Ellsworth)
BORN: February 12, 1898—Chandler, OK
DIED: October 1, 1979—Santa Monica, CA
HISTORICAL PERIOD: Modern
COMPOSITIONAL MEDIA: Orchestra, chamber music, keyboard, choral, ballet, band.
IMPORTANT ITEMS: Composed in a traditional tonal style.

Harrison, George
BORN: February 25, 1943—Liverpool
HISTORICAL PERIOD: Modern (Popular)
COMPOSITIONAL MEDIA: Popular songs.
IMPORTANT ITEMS: Lead guitar player for The Beatles. Notable songs include "Taxman," "Something" and "My Sweet Lord."

Harrison, Lou
BORN: May 14, 1917—Portland, OR
HISTORICAL PERIOD: Modern
COMPOSITIONAL MEDIA: Orchestra, chamber music, ballet, choral, opera, songs, gamelan.
IMPORTANT ITEMS: Compositions incorporate serial and aleatory techniques, Asian instruments and unusual systems of tuning.

Hassler, Hans Leo
BORN: October 26, 1564—Nuremberg, Germany
DIED: June 8, 1612—Frankfurt, Germany
HISTORICAL PERIOD: Late Renaissance
COMPOSITIONAL MEDIA: Choral, chamber music, keyboard.
IMPORTANT ITEMS: Notable works include his sacred and secular choral music.

Haydn, Franz Joseph
BORN: March 31, 1732—Rohrau, Austria
DIED: May 31, 1809—Vienna
HISTORICAL PERIOD: Classical
COMPOSITIONAL MEDIA: Orchestra, chamber music, keyboard, choral, opera, songs.
IMPORTANT ITEMS: Prolific composer, including

over 100 symphonies and numerous operas, masses, string quartets, etc.

Haydn, (Johann) Michael
BORN: September 14, 1737—Rohrau, Austria
DIED: August 10, 1806—Salzburg, Austria
HISTORICAL PERIOD: Classical
COMPOSITIONAL MEDIA: Orchestra, chamber music, keyboard, choral, opera, songs.
IMPORTANT ITEMS: Brother of Franz Joseph Haydn.

Hensel, Fanny: See Mendelssohn (-Bartholdy), Fanny Cäcilie [Hensel]

Henze, Hans Werner
BORN: July 1, 1926—Gütersloh, Germany
HISTORICAL PERIOD: Modern
COMPOSITIONAL MEDIA: Orchestra, chamber music, ballet, keyboard, choral, opera, songs.
IMPORTANT ITEMS: Compositions incorporate microtonal, twelve-tone and electronic techniques.

Herbert, Victor (August)
BORN: February 1, 1859—Dublin, Ireland
DIED: May 26, 1924—New York
HISTORICAL PERIOD: Late Romantic
COMPOSITIONAL MEDIA: Operettas, orchestra, chamber music, keyboard, songs, film, opera.
IMPORTANT ITEMS: Notable works include the operetta "Babes in Toyland."

Herrmann, Bernard
BORN: June 29, 1911—New York
DIED: December 24, 1975—Los Angeles
HISTORICAL PERIOD: Modern
COMPOSITIONAL MEDIA: Film, orchestra, chamber music, choral.
IMPORTANT ITEMS: Notable film scores include "Citizen Kane," "Psycho" and "Taxi Driver."

Hindemith, Paul
BORN: November 16, 1895—Hanau, Germany
DIED: December 28, 1963—Frankfurt, Germany
HISTORICAL PERIOD: Modern
COMPOSITIONAL MEDIA: Orchestra, chamber music, ballet, keyboard, choral, opera, band.
IMPORTANT ITEMS: A leading advocate of Gebrauchsmusik, he wrote numerous works to be played by amateurs and students. Notable compositions include "Mathis der Maler" and "Symphonic Metamorphosis on Themes of Carl Maria von Weber."

Holly, Buddy
[real name: Charles Harden Holley]
BORN: September 7, 1936—Lubbock, TX
DIED: February 2, 1959—Clear Lake, IA
HISTORICAL PERIOD: Modern (Popular)
COMPOSITIONAL MEDIA: Popular songs.
IMPORTANT ITEMS: Popular rock songwriter whose notable songs include "That'll Be the Day."

Holst, Gustav Theodore
BORN: September 21, 1874—Cheltenham, England
DIED: May 25, 1934—London
HISTORICAL PERIOD: Late Romantic
COMPOSITIONAL MEDIA: Orchestra, chamber music, ballet, keyboard, opera, songs, band.
IMPORTANT ITEMS: Professional trombonist and

organist. Notable works include the orchestral suite "The Planets."

Honegger, Arthur (Oscar)
>BORN: March 10, 1892—Le Havre, France
>DIED: November 27, 1955—Paris
>HISTORICAL PERIOD: Modern
>COMPOSITIONAL MEDIA: Orchestra, chamber music, ballet, keyboard, choral, opera, songs, film, radio.
>IMPORTANT ITEMS: A member of Les Six. Notable works include the oratorio "King David" and the orchestral composition "Pacific 231."

Hovhaness, Alan
>BORN: March 8, 1911—Somerville, MA
>HISTORICAL PERIOD: Modern
>COMPOSITIONAL MEDIA: Orchestra, chamber music, keyboard, choral, opera, band, songs, electronic.
>IMPORTANT ITEMS: Prolific composer whose compositions incorporate Armenian and Oriental modes and aleatoric techniques. Notable works include "And God Created Great Whales."

Hummel, Johann Nepomuk
>BORN: November 14, 1778—Pressburg, Germany
>DIED: October 17, 1837—Weimar, Germany
>HISTORICAL PERIOD: Classical
>COMPOSITIONAL MEDIA: Opera, chamber music, ballet, keyboard, orchestra, choral.
>IMPORTANT ITEMS: Virtuoso pianist and composer. Although well crafted, his compositions are neglected.

Humperdinck, Engelbert
>BORN: September 1, 1854—Siegburg, Germany
>DIED: September 27, 1921—Neustrelitz, Germany
>HISTORICAL PERIOD: Romantic
>COMPOSITIONAL MEDIA: Opera, orchestra, keyboard, choral, songs.
>IMPORTANT ITEMS: Notable works include the opera "Hansel and Gretel."

Husa, Karel
>BORN: August 7, 1921—Prague
>HISTORICAL PERIOD: Modern
>COMPOSITIONAL MEDIA: Orchestra, chamber music, ballet, keyboard, choral, band.
>IMPORTANT ITEMS: Became an American citizen in 1959. Awarded the Pulitzer Prize in 1969 for his third string quartet.

Ibert, Jacques (François Antoine)
>BORN: August 15, 1890—Paris
>DIED: February 5, 1962—Paris
>HISTORICAL PERIOD: Modern
>COMPOSITIONAL MEDIA: Orchestra, chamber music, ballet, keyboard, choral, opera, film.
>IMPORTANT ITEMS: Notable works include "Concerto for Flute and Orchestra" and the "Divertissement for Orchestra."

Indy, (Paul Marie Théodore) Vincent d'
>BORN: March 27, 1851—Paris
>DIED: December 2, 1931—Paris
>HISTORICAL PERIOD: Late Romantic

COMPOSITIONAL MEDIA: Orchestra, chamber music, keyboard, choral, songs.
IMPORTANT ITEMS: Co-founded the Schola Cantorum of Paris. Notable works include "Symphony on a French Mountain Air."

Ippolitov-Ivanov, Mikhail (Mikhaylovich)
BORN: November 19, 1859—Gatchina, Russia
DIED: January 28, 1935—Moscow
HISTORICAL PERIOD: Late Romantic
COMPOSITIONAL MEDIA: Orchestra, chamber music, choral, songs.
IMPORTANT ITEMS: Notable works include the symphonic suite "Caucasian Sketches."

Ireland, John (Nicholson)
BORN: August 13, 1879—Inglewood, England
DIED: June 12, 1962—Washington, England
HISTORICAL PERIOD: Late Romantic / Modern
COMPOSITIONAL MEDIA: Keyboard, orchestra, chamber music, choral, songs, band.
IMPORTANT ITEMS: His finest works are those for solo piano.

Ives, Charles (Edward)
BORN: October 20, 1874—Danbury, CT
DIED: May 19, 1954—New York
HISTORICAL PERIOD: Modern
COMPOSITIONAL MEDIA: Orchestra, chamber music, keyboard, choral, songs.
IMPORTANT ITEMS: Compositions incorporated complex rhythms, tone clusters, polytonality and aleatory techniques. Awarded the Pulitzer Prize in 1947 for his third symphony. Notable works include "The Unanswered Question" and "Three Places in New England" for chamber orchestra, "Variations on America" for organ and the "Concord Sonata" for piano.

J

Jackson, Michael
BORN: August 29, 1958—Gary, IN
HISTORICAL PERIOD: Modern (Popular)
COMPOSITIONAL MEDIA: Popular songs.
IMPORTANT ITEMS: Extremely popular singer and songwriter that began his career singing with the Jackson Five. Notable songs include "Beat It" and "Thriller."

Jacob, Gordon (Percival Septimus)
BORN: July 5, 1895—London
DIED: June 8, 1984—Saffron, Walden
HISTORICAL PERIOD: Modern
COMPOSITIONAL MEDIA: Orchestra, chamber music, ballet, songs, film.
IMPORTANT ITEMS: Composer, teacher, author and conductor.

Jagger, Mick [Michael] (Philip)
BORN: July 26, 1944—Dartford, Kent, England
HISTORICAL PERIOD: Modern (Popular)
COMPOSITIONAL MEDIA: Popular songs.
IMPORTANT ITEMS: Lead singer and songwriter for the rock group The Rolling Stones.

Janáček, Leoš
>BORN: July 3, 1854—Hukvaldy, Moravia
>DIED: August 12, 1928—Ostrau, Czechoslovakia
>HISTORICAL PERIOD: Late Romantic / Modern
>COMPOSITIONAL MEDIA: Orchestra, chamber music, keyboard, choral, opera.
>IMPORTANT ITEMS: Significant and prolific composer. Notable works include "Sinfonietta" for orchestra.

Jaques-Dalcroze: See Dalcroze, Jaques

Joel, Billy [William] (Martin)
>BORN: May 9, 1949—New York
>HISTORICAL PERIOD: Modern (Popular)
>COMPOSITIONAL MEDIA: Popular songs.
>IMPORTANT ITEMS: Popular pianist, singer and songwriter. Notable songs include "Piano Man."

John, Elton
[real name: Reginald Kenneth Dwight]
>BORN: March 25, 1947—Middlesex, England
>HISTORICAL PERIOD: Modern (Popular)
>COMPOSITIONAL MEDIA: Popular songs, film.
>IMPORTANT ITEMS: Highly successful pianist, singer and songwriter. Notable works include the song "Rocket Man" and five songs for the film "The Lion King."

Johnson, Robert
>BORN: May 8, 1911—Hazlehurst, MS
>DIED: August 16, 1938—Greenwood, MS
>HISTORICAL PERIOD: Modern (Popular)
>COMPOSITIONAL MEDIA: Popular songs.
>IMPORTANT ITEMS: Legendary blues guitarist and songwriter. Notable songs include "Cross Road Blues."

Jones, Quincy (Delight, Jr.)
>BORN: March 14, 1933—Chicago, IL
>HISTORICAL PERIOD: Modern (Popular)
>COMPOSITIONAL MEDIA: Popular songs, instrumental jazz, film.
>IMPORTANT ITEMS: Professional jazz trumpeter, composer, conductor and record producer. Notable works include the film score "The Color Purple."

Joplin, Scott
>BORN: November 24, 1868—Marshall, TX
>DIED: April 1, 1917—New York
>HISTORICAL PERIOD: Late Romantic (Popular)
>COMPOSITIONAL MEDIA: Keyboard, opera.
>IMPORTANT ITEMS: Notable works include ragtime piano pieces "Maple Leaf Rag" and "The Entertainer."

Josquin des Prez: See des Pres, Josquin

K

Kabalevsky, Dmitri (Borisovich)
>BORN: December 30, 1904—St. Petersburg, Russia
>DIED: February 14, 1987—Moscow
>HISTORICAL PERIOD: Modern
>COMPOSITIONAL MEDIA: Orchestra, chamber music, keyboard, choral, opera, songs, film.
>IMPORTANT ITEMS: Notable works include the

orchestral suite "The Comedians" and numerous piano pieces for children.

Kagel, Mauricio
>BORN: December 24, 1931—Buenos Aires, Argentina
>HISTORICAL PERIOD: Modern
>COMPOSITIONAL MEDIA: Chamber music, keyboard, electronic, choral, film.
>IMPORTANT ITEMS: Compositions incorporate aleatory, electronic, tape and audio-visual techniques.

Kay, Ulysses (Simpson)
>BORN: January 7, 1917—Tucson, AR
>DIED: May 20, 1995—Englewood, NJ
>HISTORICAL PERIOD: Modern
>COMPOSITIONAL MEDIA: Orchestra, chamber music, ballet, keyboard, choral, opera, songs, film, band.
>IMPORTANT ITEMS: Prolific composer and teacher.

Kern, Jerome (David)
>BORN: January 27, 1885—New York
>DIED: November 11, 1945—New York
>HISTORICAL PERIOD: Modern (Popular)
>COMPOSITIONAL MEDIA: Popular songs, musicals.
>IMPORTANT ITEMS: Notable works include the Broadway musical "Showboat" which includes the song "Ol' Man River."

Khachaturian, Aram (llich)
>BORN: June 6, 1903—Tiflis, Russia
>DIED: May 1, 1978—Moscow
>HISTORICAL PERIOD: Modern
>COMPOSITIONAL MEDIA: Orchestra, chamber music, ballet, keyboard, choral, film.
>IMPORTANT ITEMS: Notable works include "Sabre Dance" from the ballet "Gayane."

King, Carl L.
>BORN: February 21, 1891—Painterville, OH
>DIED: March 31, 1971—Fort Dodge, IA
>HISTORICAL PERIOD: Late Romantic (Popular)
>COMPOSITIONAL MEDIA: Band.
>IMPORTANT ITEMS: Most popular marches include "Barnum & Bailey's Favorite." His music inspired the musical "The Music Man."

King, Carole (real name: Klein)
>BORN: February 9, 1941—New York
>HISTORICAL PERIOD: Modern (Popular)
>COMPOSITIONAL MEDIA: Popular songs.
>IMPORTANT ITEMS: Notable songs include "Up on the Roof" and "Take Good Care of My Baby."

Kodály, Zoltán
>BORN: December 16, 1882—Kecskemét, Hungary
>DIED: March 6, 1967—Budapest, Hungary
>HISTORICAL PERIOD: Modern
>COMPOSITIONAL MEDIA: Orchestra, chamber music, keyboard, choral, opera, songs.
>IMPORTANT ITEMS: Worked with Bartok in collecting folksongs. Notable works include the orchestral suite "Háry János" from the opera of the same name.

Köhler, Louis
>BORN: September 5, 1820—Brunswick, Germany
>DIED: February 16, 1886—Königsberg, Germany
>HISTORICAL PERIOD: Romantic
>COMPOSITIONAL MEDIA: Orchestra, ballet, choral,

opera.
IMPORTANT ITEMS: His methods for piano are still used today.

Korngold, Erich Wolfgang
BORN: May 29, 1897—Brno, Austria
DIED: November 29, 1957—Hollywood, CA
HISTORICAL PERIOD: Modern
COMPOSITIONAL MEDIA: Orchestra, opera, film, chamber music, keyboard, songs.
IMPORTANT ITEMS: Prolific composer of concert music and film scores.

Kraft, William
BORN: September 6, 1923—Chicago, IL
HISTORICAL PERIOD: Modern
COMPOSITIONAL MEDIA: Orchestra, chamber music, choral, theatrical, film, radio.
IMPORTANT ITEMS: Professional percussionist, composer and conductor.

Kreisler, Fritz (Friedrich)
BORN: February 2, 1875—Vienna
DIED: January 29, 1962—New York
HISTORICAL PERIOD: Late Romantic
COMPOSITIONAL MEDIA: Chamber music, operettas, violin.
IMPORTANT ITEMS: Virtuoso violinist who composed many violin pieces, some of which he first attributed to other composers.

Krenek, Ernst
BORN: August 23, 1900—Vienna
DIED: December 22, 1991—Palm Springs, CA
HISTORICAL PERIOD: Modern
COMPOSITIONAL MEDIA: Orchestra, chamber music, ballet, keyboard, choral, opera, electronic.
IMPORTANT ITEMS: Notable works include the opera "Jonny spielt auf" which incorporates jazz.

Kubik, Gail (Thompson)
BORN: September 5, 1914—S. Coffeyville, OK
DIED: July 20, 1984—Covina, CA
HISTORICAL PERIOD: Modern
COMPOSITIONAL MEDIA: Orchestra, chamber music, ballet, keyboard, choral, opera, songs, film.
IMPORTANT ITEMS: Awarded the Pulitzer Prize in 1952 for his "Symphonie Concertante" for piano, viola, trumpet and orchestra.

Kuhlau, (Daniel) Friedrick (Rudolph)
BORN: September 11, 1786—Ülzen, Germany
DIED: March 12, 1832—Copenhagen, Denmark
HISTORICAL PERIOD: Late Classical/Early Romantic
COMPOSITIONAL MEDIA: Keyboard, chamber music, choral, songs, theatrical.
IMPORTANT ITEMS: Notable works include instructional piano pieces.

Kuhnau, Johann
BORN: April 6, 1660—Geising, Saxony
DIED: June 5, 1722—Leipzig, Germany
HISTORICAL PERIOD: Baroque
COMPOSITIONAL MEDIA: Keyboard, choral.
IMPORTANT ITEMS: Organist, author and composer.

L

Lalo, Édouard (-Victor-Antoine)
BORN: January 27, 1823—Lille, France
DIED: April 22, 1892—Paris
HISTORICAL PERIOD: Romantic
COMPOSITIONAL MEDIA: Orchestra, chamber music, ballet, keyboard, choral, opera, songs.
IMPORTANT ITEMS: Notable works include "Symphonie espagnole."

Landini, Francesco
BORN: c. 1325—Florence
DIED: September 2, 1397—Florence
HISTORICAL PERIOD: Medieval
COMPOSITIONAL MEDIA: Vocal, choral.
IMPORTANT ITEMS: Became blind as a child. The Landini cadence is named after him.

Lasso, Orlando di
[other spellings: Orlandus Lassus or Roland de Lassus]
BORN: 1532—Mons, Belgium
DIED: June 14, 1594—Munich, Germany
HISTORICAL PERIOD: Renaissance
COMPOSITIONAL MEDIA: Choral, songs.
IMPORTANT ITEMS: Composed more than 2,000 works. Notable works include his Italian madrigals, Latin motets, French chansons, and German lieder.

Lauridsen, Morten (Johannes)
BORN: February 27, 1943—Colfax, WA
HISTORICAL PERIOD: Modern
COMPOSITIONAL MEDIA: Choral, songs, chamber music.
IMPORTANT ITEMS: Award winning composer and teacher. Notable works include the song cycles "Mid-Winter Songs" and "Madrigali."

Lecuona, Ernesto
BORN: August 7, 1896—Havana, Cuba
DIED: November 29, 1963—Santa Cruz de Tenerife, Canary Islands
HISTORICAL PERIOD: Modern (Popular)
COMPOSITIONAL MEDIA: Popular songs.
IMPORTANT ITEMS: Notable songs include "Malagueña."

Lehar, Franz
BORN: April 30, 1870—Komorn, Hungary
DIED: October 24, 1948—Bad Ischl, Austria
HISTORICAL PERIOD: Modern (Popular)
COMPOSITIONAL MEDIA: Orchestra, keyboard, operettas, popular songs, film, band.
IMPORTANT ITEMS: Best remembered for the operetta "The Merry Widow."

Lennon, John (Winston Ono)
BORN: October 9, 1940—Liverpool, England
DIED: December 8, 1980—New York
HISTORICAL PERIOD: Modern (Popular)
COMPOSITIONAL MEDIA: Popular songs, film.
IMPORTANT ITEMS: Brilliant songwriter and member of the rock group The Beatles. As a member of The Beatles, he co-wrote, with Paul McCartney, such songs as "A Hard Day's Night," "Help," "In My Life," "Norwegian Wood" and "Strawberry Fields Forever." Later he wrote "Imagine," "Cold Turkey" and "(Just Like) Starting Over."

Leoncavallo, Ruggiero
BORN: April 23, 1857—Naples
DIED: August 9, 1919—Montecatini, Italy
HISTORICAL PERIOD: Romantic
COMPOSITIONAL MEDIA: Opera, orchestra, ballet, keyboard, operettas, songs.
IMPORTANT ITEMS: Notable works include the opera "Pagliacci."

Léonin [Leoninus]
BORN: c. 1135—Paris
DIED: c. 1201—Paris
HISTORICAL PERIOD: Medieval
COMPOSITIONAL MEDIA: Choral.
IMPORTANT ITEMS: Ars antiqua composer of organum for the Cathedral of Notre Dame.

Lewis, John
BORN: May 3, 1920—La Grange, IL
HISTORICAL PERIOD: Modern
COMPOSITIONAL MEDIA: Instrumental jazz, film, popular songs, ballet.
IMPORTANT ITEMS: Founded the "Modern Jazz Quartet" in 1952. Incorporates elements of classical and jazz styles in his compositions.

Ligeti, Gyorgy (Sándor)
BORN: May 28, 1923—Dicsöszentmarton, Hungary
HISTORICAL PERIOD: Modern
COMPOSITIONAL MEDIA: Orchestra, choral, keyboard, chamber music, opera.
IMPORTANT ITEMS: Frequent use of tone clusters and dense scoring. The Kyrie from his Requiem was featured in the soundtrack of "2001: A Space Odyssey."

Linn, Robert
BORN: August 11, 1925—San Francisco, CA
HISTORICAL PERIOD: Modern
COMPOSITIONAL MEDIA: Orchestra, chamber music, band, songs.
IMPORTANT ITEMS: Award winning composer and teacher. Studied with Darius Milhaud, Halsey Stevens, Roger Sessions and Ingolf Dahl.

Liszt, Franz
BORN: October 22, 1811—Raiding, Hungary
DIED: July 31, 1886—Bayreuth, Germany
HISTORICAL PERIOD: Romantic
COMPOSITIONAL MEDIA: Keyboard, orchestra, chamber music, choral, opera, songs.
IMPORTANT ITEMS: Professional pianist and composer whose notable works include "Hungarian Rhapsodies," two piano concertos, the symphonic poem "Les Préludes" and numerous piano pieces including "Liebesträume."

Lloyd Webber, Andrew
BORN: March 22, 1948—London
HISTORICAL PERIOD: Modern (Popular)
COMPOSITIONAL MEDIA: Musicals, orchestra, choral, film.
IMPORTANT ITEMS: Tremendously popular musicals including "Jesus Christ Superstar," "Evita," "Cats" and "Phantom of the Opera."

Loesser, Frank (Henry)
BORN: June 29, 1910—New York
DIED: July 28, 1969—New York
HISTORICAL PERIOD: Modern (Popular)
COMPOSITIONAL MEDIA: Musicals, popular songs.
IMPORTANT ITEMS: Notable works include the Broadway musicals "Guys and Dolls" and "How to Succeed in Business Without Really Trying."

Loewe, Frederick
BORN: June 10, 1901—Vienna
DIED: February 14, 1988—Palm Springs, CA
HISTORICAL PERIOD: Modern (Popular)
COMPOSITIONAL MEDIA: Musicals, popular songs.
IMPORTANT ITEMS: Notable works include the Broadway musicals "My Fair Lady," "Brigadoon" and "Camelot."

Luening, Otto (Clarence)
BORN: June 15, 1900—Milwaukee, WI
HISTORICAL PERIOD: Modern
COMPOSITIONAL MEDIA: Orchestra, chamber music, ballet, keyboard, choral, opera, songs, electronic.
IMPORTANT ITEMS: Compositions incorporate tape and electronic techniques. Collaborated with Vladimir Ussachevsky.

Lully, Jean-Baptiste
BORN: November 28, 1632—Florence, Italy
DIED: March 22, 1687—Paris
HISTORICAL PERIOD: Baroque
COMPOSITIONAL MEDIA: Opera, chamber music, ballet, choral, songs, theatrical.
IMPORTANT ITEMS: Developed the French overture. Notable works include the opera "Le Bourgeois Gentilhomme."

Lutoslawski, Witold
BORN: January 25, 1913—Warsaw
DIED: February 7, 1994—Warsaw
HISTORICAL PERIOD: Modern
COMPOSITIONAL MEDIA: Orchestra, chamber music, keyboard, choral, songs, theatrical, film, radio.
IMPORTANT ITEMS: Award winning composer of well-crafted music. Texture is an important element of his compositions.

MacDowell, Edward (Alexander)
BORN: December 18, 1860—New York
DIED: January 23, 1908—New York
HISTORICAL PERIOD: Romantic
COMPOSITIONAL MEDIA: Keyboard, orchestra, choral, songs.
IMPORTANT ITEMS: Prolific composer whose notable works include the piano piece "To a Wild Rose" from "Woodland Sketches."

Machaut, Guillaume de
BORN: c.1300—Machaut, Champagne, France
DIED: April 1377—Rheims, France
HISTORICAL PERIOD: Medieval
COMPOSITIONAL MEDIA: Choral.

IMPORTANT ITEMS: One of the most important ars nova composers. His "Messe de Notre Dame" for four voices is one of the earliest complete polyphonic settings of the Mass.

Mahler, Gustav
BORN: July 7, 1860—Kalischt, Bohemia
DIED: May 18, 1911—Vienna
HISTORICAL PERIOD: Late Romantic
COMPOSITIONAL MEDIA: Orchestra, choral, songs, keyboard, chamber music.
IMPORTANT ITEMS: Notable works include ten large-scale symphonies and the song cycle "Kindertotenlieder."

Mancini, Henry
BORN: April 16, 1924—Cleveland, OH
DIED: June 14, 1994—Beverly Hills, CA
HISTORICAL PERIOD: Modern (Popular)
COMPOSITIONAL MEDIA: Popular songs, film, TV.
IMPORTANT ITEMS: Notable works include the film scores "Breakfast at Tiffany's" and "The Pink Panther."

Marenzio, Luca
BORN: c.1553—Coccaglio, Bresica, Italy
DIED: August 22, 1599—Rome
HISTORICAL PERIOD: Renaissance
COMPOSITIONAL MEDIA: Choral.
IMPORTANT ITEMS: Best known as a composer of madrigals.

Martin, Frank
BORN: September 15, 1890—Geneva, Switzerland
DIED: November 21, 1974—Naarden, the Netherlands
HISTORICAL PERIOD: Modern
COMPOSITIONAL MEDIA: Orchestra, chamber music, ballet, keyboard, choral, opera, songs.
IMPORTANT ITEMS: Compositions incorporate folk song materials and twelve-tone techniques.

Martino, Donald (James)
BORN: May 16, 1931—Plainfield, NJ
HISTORICAL PERIOD: Modern
COMPOSITIONAL MEDIA: Chamber music, orchestra, choral, keyboard, songs, electronic.
IMPORTANT ITEMS: Awarded the Pulitzer Prize in 1974 for his chamber piece, "Notturno."

Martinů, Bohuslav
BORN: December 8, 1890—Polička, Czech
DIED: August 28, 1959—Basel, Switzerland
HISTORICAL PERIOD: Modern
COMPOSITIONAL MEDIA: Orchestra, opera, ballet, chamber music, choral.
IMPORTANT ITEMS: Influenced by Bohemian folk music, neoclassicism and impressionism.

Mascagni, Pietro
BORN: December 7, 1863—Livorno, Italy
DIED: August 2, 1945—Rome
HISTORICAL PERIOD: Late Romantic/Modern
COMPOSITIONAL MEDIA: Opera, chamber music, choral, songs, keyboard.
IMPORTANT ITEMS: Notable works include the opera "Cavalleria rusticana."

Massenet, Jules (-Émile-Frédéric)
BORN: May 12, 1842—Montaud, France
DIED: August 13, 1912—Paris

HISTORICAL PERIOD: Romantic
COMPOSITIONAL MEDIA: Opera, orchestra, choral, chamber music, ballet, keyboard, songs.
IMPORTANT ITEMS: Notable works include the opera "Manon."

Mayuzumi, Toshiro
BORN: February 20, 1929—Yokohama, Japan
HISTORICAL PERIOD: Modern
COMPOSITIONAL MEDIA: Orchestra, chamber music, ballet, choral, opera, electronic, film.
IMPORTANT ITEMS: Compositions incorporate traditional Japanese music, electronic sounds and serial techniques.

McCartney, (John) Paul
BORN: June 18, 1942—Liverpool, England
HISTORICAL PERIOD: Modern (Popular)
COMPOSITIONAL MEDIA: Popular songs, film, choral.
IMPORTANT ITEMS: Popular songwriter and member of the rock group The Beatles. As a member of the Beatles, he co-wrote, with John Lennon, such songs as "Michelle," "Eleanor Rigby" and "Yesterday." In 1991 he premiered his "Liverpool Oratorio."

Mendelssohn (-Bartholdy), Fanny Cäecilie [married name: Hensel]
BORN: November 14, 1805—Hamburg
DIED: May 14, 1847—Berlin
HISTORICAL PERIOD: Romantic
COMPOSITIONAL MEDIA: Songs, chamber music, choral, keyboard.
IMPORTANT ITEMS: Talented pianist and composer; sister of Felix Mendelssohn.

Mendelssohn (-Bartholdy), Felix
BORN: February 3, 1809—Hamburg, Germany
DIED: November 4, 1847—Leipzig, Germany
HISTORICAL PERIOD: Romantic
COMPOSITIONAL MEDIA: Orchestra, chamber music, keyboard, choral, opera, songs, theatrical.
IMPORTANT ITEMS: A prolific composer whose notable works include incidental music to Shakespeare's "A Midsummer Night's Dream," the oratorio "Elijah," the "Hebrides" overture and violin concerto.

Mennin, Peter [real name: Peter Mennini]
BORN: May 17, 1923—Erie, PA
DIED: June 17, 1983—New York
HISTORICAL PERIOD: Modern
COMPOSITIONAL MEDIA: Orchestra, chamber music, keyboard, choral, songs.
IMPORTANT ITEMS: Award winning composer and president of the Juilliard School.

Menotti, Gian Carlo
BORN: July 7, 1911—Cadegliano, Italy
HISTORICAL PERIOD: Modern
COMPOSITIONAL MEDIA: Opera, orchestra, ballet, keyboard, songs, film, radio, TV.
IMPORTANT ITEMS: Awarded the Pulitzer Prize for "The Consul." Notable works include the opera "Amahl and the Night Visitors."

Messiaen, Olivier (Eugéne Prosper Charles)
BORN: December 10, 1908—Avignon, France
DIED: April 28, 1992—Clichy, Hauts-de Seine, France

HISTORICAL PERIOD: Modern
COMPOSITIONAL MEDIA: Orchestra, chamber music, keyboard, opera, songs.
IMPORTANT ITEMS: Highly influential composer and teacher. Pupils included Boulez, Stockhausen and Xenakis. Compositions incorporate extra musical sources (such as bird songs), Gregorian chant and oriental rhythms. Notable works include "Quatuor pour la fin du temps" and "Turàngalîla-Symphonie."

Meyerbeer, Giacomo
[real name: Jakob Liebmann Beer]
BORN: September 5, 1791—Berlin, Germany
DIED: May 2, 1864—Paris
HISTORICAL PERIOD: Romantic
COMPOSITIONAL MEDIA: Opera, chamber music, choral, orchestra, songs.
IMPORTANT ITEMS: Notable works include the opera "Les Huguenots."

Milhaud, Darius
BORN: September 4, 1892—Aix-en-Provence, France
DIED: June 22, 1974—Geneva, Switzerland
HISTORICAL PERIOD: Modern
COMPOSITIONAL MEDIA: Orchestra, chamber music, ballet, keyboard, choral, opera, songs, theatrical, film.
IMPORTANT ITEMS: Many of his compositions use polytonality. Notable works include the ballet "La Création du monde" which incorporates blues and jazz. A member of Les Six.

Mingus, Charles
BORN: April 22, 1922—Nogales, AZ
DIED: January 8, 1979—Cuernavaca, Mexico
HISTORICAL PERIOD: Modern (Jazz)
COMPOSITIONAL MEDIA: Songs, instrumental jazz, film.
IMPORTANT ITEMS: Professional jazz bassist whose notable works include "Epitaph" for 30 instruments.

Monk, Thelonious
BORN: October 10, 1918—Rock Mountain, NC
DIED: February 17, 1982—Weehawken, NJ
HISTORICAL PERIOD: Modern (Jazz)
COMPOSITIONAL MEDIA: Instrumental jazz.
IMPORTANT ITEMS: Professional jazz pianist whose notable works include "Round Midnight."

Monteverdi, Claudio (Giovanni Antonio)
BORN: May 15, 1567—Cremona, Italy
DIED: November 29, 1643—Venice
HISTORICAL PERIOD: Late Renaissance
COMPOSITIONAL MEDIA: Opera, ballet, choral, songs.
IMPORTANT ITEMS: The first important composer of operas. Notable works include "Ariadne's Lament" from the opera "L'Arianna," and the operas "Orfeo" and "L'Incaronazione di Poppea."

Moore, Douglas (Stuart)
BORN: August 10, 1893—Cutchogue, NY
DIED: July 25, 1969—Greenport, NY
HISTORICAL PERIOD: Modern
COMPOSITIONAL MEDIA: Opera, orchestra, chamber music, choral, songs.
IMPORTANT ITEMS: Notable works include the opera "Ballad of Baby Doe."

Morley, Thomas
>BORN: c. 1557—Norwich, England
>DIED: October, 1602—London
>HISTORICAL PERIOD: Renaissance
>COMPOSITIONAL MEDIA: Choral, songs, chamber music.
>IMPORTANT ITEMS: Notable works include his numerous madrigals and lute music.

Morton, Ferdinand "Jelly Roll"
>BORN: October 20, 1890—New Orleans
>DIED: July 10, 1941—Los Angeles
>HISTORICAL PERIOD: Modern (Jazz)
>COMPOSITIONAL MEDIA: Popular instrumental jazz.
>IMPORTANT ITEMS: An early pioneer of jazz arranging. Notable works include "Jelly Roll Blues."

Mouret, Jean-Joseph
>BORN: April 11, 1682—Avignon, France
>DIED: December 20, 1738—Charenton, France
>HISTORICAL PERIOD: Baroque
>COMPOSITIONAL MEDIA: Opera, ballet, choral, orchestra.
>IMPORTANT ITEMS: Notable works include his "Rondeau" which is used as the theme of the TV program "Masterpiece Theatre."

Mozart, (Johann Georg) Leopold
>BORN: November 14, 1719—Augsburg, Austria
>DIED: May 28, 1787—Salzburg, Austria
>HISTORICAL PERIOD: Early Classical
>COMPOSITIONAL MEDIA: Chamber music, keyboard, choral, opera, songs.
>IMPORTANT ITEMS: Father of W.A. Mozart whose most popular work is his "Toy Symphony."

Mozart, Wolfgang Amadeus
>BORN: January 27, 1756—Salzburg, Austria
>DIED: December 5, 1791—Vienna
>HISTORICAL PERIOD: Classical
>COMPOSITIONAL MEDIA: Orchestra, chamber music, keyboard, choral, opera, ballet, songs.
>IMPORTANT ITEMS: One of the most important composers of the classical period. A very prolific composer who wrote over 600 pieces during his short lifetime. Notable works include 41 symphonies, 27 piano concertos, the "Requiem" in D minor, "Eine Kleine Nachtmusik" for strings, and the operas "Don Giovanni" and "The Magic Flute."

Mussorgsky, Modest (Petrovich)
>BORN: March 21, 1839—Karevo, Russia
>DIED: March 28, 1881—St. Petersburg, Russia
>HISTORICAL PERIOD: Romantic
>COMPOSITIONAL MEDIA: Opera, orchestra, keyboard, choral, songs.
>IMPORTANT ITEMS: Notable works include the orchestral composition "Night on Bald Mountain," the piano piece "Pictures at an Exhibition" (which is best known in the version orchestrated by Ravel) and the opera "Boris Godunov."

Nelhybel, Vaclav
BORN: September 24, 1919—Polanka, Czechoslovakia
DIED: March 22, 1996—Scranton, PA
HISTORICAL PERIOD: Modern
COMPOSITIONAL MEDIA: Orchestra, chamber music, choral, ballet, keyboard, opera, band.
IMPORTANT ITEMS: Notable works include his numerous works for symphonic band.

Newman, Alfred
BORN: March 17, 1900—New Haven, CT
DIED: February 17, 1970—Los Angeles
HISTORICAL PERIOD: Modern
COMPOSITIONAL MEDIA: Film.
IMPORTANT ITEMS: Award winning film composer. Notable scores include "The Hunchback of Notre Dame" (1939) and "Wuthering Heights."

Nicolai, (Carl) Otto (Ehrenfried)
BORN: June 9, 1810—Königsberg, Germany
DIED: May 11, 1849—Berlin, Germany
HISTORICAL PERIOD: Romantic
COMPOSITIONAL MEDIA: Orchestra, opera, chamber music, keyboard, choral, songs.
IMPORTANT ITEMS: Notable works include the opera "The Merry Wives of Windsor."

Nielsen, Carl (August)
BORN: June 9, 1865—Nøre-Lyndelse, Denmark
DIED: October 3, 1931—Copenhagen, Denmark
HISTORICAL PERIOD: Late Romantic
COMPOSITIONAL MEDIA: Orchestra, choral, chamber music, keyboard, opera, songs, theatrical.
IMPORTANT ITEMS: Notable works include six symphonies.

Nilsson, Bo
BORN: May 1, 1937—Skelleftehamn, Sweden
HISTORICAL PERIOD: Modern
COMPOSITIONAL MEDIA: Chamber music, orchestra, keyboard, electronic.
IMPORTANT ITEMS: Compositions incorporate serial and electronic techniques.

Nono, Luigi
BORN: January 29, 1924—Venice
DIED: May 8, 1990—Venice
HISTORICAL PERIOD: Modern
COMPOSITIONAL MEDIA: Orchestra, chamber music, ballet, keyboard, choral, opera, songs, electronic.
IMPORTANT ITEMS: Compositions incorporate tape, electronic and serial techniques.

Nordoff, Paul
BORN: June 4, 1900—Philadelphia, PA
DIED: January 18, 1977—Herdecke, Germany
HISTORICAL PERIOD: Modern
COMPOSITIONAL MEDIA: Orchestra, chamber music, ballet, opera.
IMPORTANT ITEMS: Specialized in music therapy of handicapped children.

O

Obrecht, Jacob
BORN: November 22, 1450—Bergen-op-Zoom, Netherlands
DIED: c. 1505—Ferrara, Italy
HISTORICAL PERIOD: Renaissance
COMPOSITIONAL MEDIA: Choral, songs.
IMPORTANT ITEMS: A master of the Flemish school best remembered for religious motets and Masses.

Ockeghem, Johannes
BORN: c. 1410
DIED: February 6, 1497—Tours, France
HISTORICAL PERIOD: Early Renaissance
COMPOSITIONAL MEDIA: Choral, songs.
IMPORTANT ITEMS: Composed numerous Masses. His Requiem is the earliest surviving polyphonic example of this form.

Offenbach, Jacques
BORN: June 20, 1819—Cologne, Germany
DIED: October 5, 1880—Paris
HISTORICAL PERIOD: Romantic
COMPOSITIONAL MEDIA: Operettas, opera, ballet, chamber music.
IMPORTANT ITEMS: Notable works include the opera "The Tales of Hoffmann," and the cancan from from the operetta "Orpheus in the Underworld."

Orff, Carl
BORN: July 10, 1895—Munich, Germany
DIED: March 29, 1982—Munich, Germany
HISTORICAL PERIOD: Modern
COMPOSITIONAL MEDIA: Orchestra, choral, opera, chamber music.
IMPORTANT ITEMS: Notable works include the oratorio "Carmina burana." Was active in teaching music to young children throughout his life.

P

Pachelbel, Johann
BORN: September 1, 1653—Nuremberg, Germany
DIED: March 3, 1706—Nuremberg, Germany
HISTORICAL PERIOD: Baroque
COMPOSITIONAL MEDIA: Keyboard, chamber music, choral.
IMPORTANT ITEMS: Notable works include the "Canon and Gigue" in D.

Paderewski, Ignace (Jan)
BORN: November 18, 1860—Kurylowka, Russia
DIED: June 29, 1941—New York
HISTORICAL PERIOD: Romantic
COMPOSITIONAL MEDIA: Keyboard, orchestra, opera, songs.
IMPORTANT ITEMS: World-famous pianist and composer.

Paganini, Niccolò
>BORN: October 27, 1782—Genoa, Italy
>DIED: May 27, 1840—Nice, France
>HISTORICAL PERIOD: Romantic
>COMPOSITIONAL MEDIA: Violin, chamber music, orchestra.
>IMPORTANT ITEMS: Virtuoso violinist whose notable works include "24 Caprices" for solo violin and six violin concertos.

Palestrina, Giovanni Pierluigi da
>BORN: c. 1525—Palestrina, Italy
>DIED: February 2, 1594—Rome
>HISTORICAL PERIOD: Renaissance
>COMPOSITIONAL MEDIA: Choral, songs.
>IMPORTANT ITEMS: Notable works include Masses, motets and other polyphonic sacred music.

Palmer, Willard A.
>BORN: January 31, 1917—McComb, MS
>DIED: April 30, 1996—Houston, TX
>HISTORICAL PERIOD: Modern
>COMPOSITIONAL MEDIA: Accordion, keyboard.
>IMPORTANT ITEMS: Substantial contributor to superb accordion and piano methods and highly respected editor of piano repertoire.

Parker, Horatio (William)
>BORN: September 15, 1863—Auburndale, MA
>DIED: December 18, 1919—Cedarhurst, NY
>HISTORICAL PERIOD: Romantic
>COMPOSITIONAL MEDIA: Choral, orchestra, chamber music, keyboard, opera, songs.
>IMPORTANT ITEMS: Award winning composer and teacher of Charles Ives.

Partch, Harry
>BORN: June 24, 1901—Oakland, CA
>DIED: September 3, 1974—San Diego, CA
>HISTORICAL PERIOD: Modern
>COMPOSITIONAL MEDIA: Chamber music, theatrical, choral, film.
>IMPORTANT ITEMS: Developed numerous musical instruments, some of which use a scale consisting of 43 tones to the octave.

Peeters, Flor
>BORN: July 4, 1903—Thielen, Belgium
>DIED: July 4, 1986—Antwerp, Belgium
>HISTORICAL PERIOD: Modern
>COMPOSITIONAL MEDIA: Keyboard, choral, songs.
>IMPORTANT ITEMS: Professional organist and composer best known for his numerous works for organ.

Penderecki, Krzysztof
>BORN: November 23, 1933—Debica, Poland
>HISTORICAL PERIOD: Modern
>COMPOSITIONAL MEDIA: Orchestra, chamber music, choral, opera, songs.
>IMPORTANT ITEMS: Compositions incorporate graphic notation. Notable works include "Threnody to the Victims of Hiroshima" for string orchestra.

Pergolesi, Giovanni Battista
>BORN: January 4, 1710—Jesi, Italy
>DIED: March 16, 1736—Pozzuoli, Italy
>HISTORICAL PERIOD: Baroque

COMPOSITIONAL MEDIA: Opera, chamber music, keyboard, choral.
IMPORTANT ITEMS: Notable works include the intermezzo "La Serva padrona."

Peri, Jacopo
BORN: August 20, 1561—Rome
DIED: August 12, 1633—Florence
HISTORICAL PERIOD: Baroque
COMPOSITIONAL GENRE(S): Opera, choral, ballet, songs.
IMPORTANT ITEMS: Notable for what is considered the first opera, "Dafne."

Perle, George
BORN: May 6, 1915—Bayonne, NJ
HISTORICAL PERIOD: Modern
COMPOSITIONAL MEDIA: Orchestra, chamber music, keyboard, choral.
IMPORTANT ITEMS: Compositions incorporate twelve-tone techniques. Awarded the Pulitzer Prize for his "Wind Quintet No. 4."

Perotin [Perotinus]
BORN: c. 1155-1160
DIED: c. 1200-1205
HISTORICAL PERIOD: Medieval
COMPOSITIONAL MEDIA: Choral.
IMPORTANT ITEMS: French ars antiqua composer of sacred music for the Cathedral of Notre Dame.

Persichetti, Vincent (Ludwig)
BORN: June 6, 1915—Philadelphia, PA
DIED: August 13, 1987—Philadelphia, PA
HISTORICAL PERIOD: Modern
COMPOSITIONAL MEDIA: Orchestra, chamber music, keyboard, choral, songs, band.
IMPORTANT ITEMS: Prolific composer, conductor and teacher.

Pezel [Petzel], Johann Christoph
BORN: December 5,1639—Glatz, Germany
DIED: October 13, 1694—Bautzen, Germany
HISTORICAL PERIOD: Baroque
COMPOSITIONAL MEDIA: Chamber music, choral.
IMPORTANT ITEMS: A prolific composer of music for wind instruments.

Piccinni, Niccolo
BORN: January 16, 1728—Bari, Italy
DIED: May 7, 1800—Passy, France
HISTORICAL PERIOD: Classical
COMPOSITIONAL MEDIA: Opera.
IMPORTANT ITEMS: Prolific composer of opera who was a rival, yet still an admirer, of Gluck.

Pinkham, Daniel (Rogers, Jr.)
BORN: June 5, 1923—Lynn, MA
HISTORICAL PERIOD: Modern
COMPOSITIONAL MEDIA: Choral, orchestra, chamber music, keyboard, opera, electronic.
IMPORTANT ITEMS: Compositions are neo-classical as well as incorporating tape and electronic techniques.

Piston, Walter (Hamor, Jr.)
BORN: January 20, 1894—Rockland, ME
DIED: November 12, 1976—Belmont, MA

HISTORICAL PERIOD: Modern
COMPOSITIONAL MEDIA: Orchestra, chamber music, keyboard, choral, ballet.
IMPORTANT ITEMS: Award winning composer and teacher. Pupils included Adler, Bernstein and Carter. Awarded the Pulizter Prize twice for "Symphony No. 3" and "Symphony No. 7."

Ponchielli, Amilcare
BORN: August 31, 1834—Paderno, Italy
DIED: January 15, 1886—Milan
HISTORICAL PERIOD: Romantic
COMPOSITIONAL MEDIA: Opera, orchestra, band, chamber music, choral, keyboard.
IMPORTANT ITEMS: Notable works include "Dance of the Hours" from the opera "La Gioconda."

Porter, Cole (Albert)
BORN: June 9, 1891—Peru, IN
DIED: October 15, 1964—Santa Monica, CA
HISTORICAL PERIOD: Modern (Popular)
COMPOSITIONAL MEDIA: Popular songs, musicals, film.
IMPORTANT ITEMS: Notable works include the Broadway musical "Kiss Me Kate" and the songs "Begin the Beguine" and "Let's Do It."

Poulenc, Francis (Jean Marcel)
BORN: January 7, 1899—Paris
DIED: January 30, 1963—Paris
HISTORICAL PERIOD: Modern
COMPOSITIONAL MEDIA: Orchestra, choral, chamber music, ballet, keyboard, opera, songs, guitar, film.
IMPORTANT ITEMS: A member of Les Six. Notable works include the sacred choral works "Stabat Mater" and "Gloria," and the opera "Les Dialogues des Carmélites."

Powell, Mel
[real name: Melvin Epstein]
BORN: February 12, 1923—New York
HISTORICAL PERIOD: Modern
COMPOSITIONAL MEDIA: Chamber music, orchestra, keyboard, choral, electronic.
IMPORTANT ITEMS: Professional jazz pianist who later turned to serious composition. Awarded the Pulitzer Prize in 1990 for "Duplicates," a concerto for two pianos and orchestra.

Praetorius, Michael
BORN: February 15, 1571—Kreuzberg, Germany
DIED: February 15, 1621—Wolfenbüttel, Germany
HISTORICAL PERIOD: Renaissance
COMPOSITIONAL MEDIA: Choral, chamber music.
IMPORTANT ITEMS: Prolific composer best known for his sacred choral music.

Prokofiev, Sergei Sergeievich
BORN: April 27, 1891—Sontzovka, Russia
DIED: March 5, 1953—Moscow
HISTORICAL PERIOD: Modern
COMPOSITIONAL MEDIA: Orchestra, chamber music, opera, ballet, keyboard, choral, film.
IMPORTANT ITEMS: Highly prolific composer. Notable works include the opera "Love of Three Oranges," the cantata "Alexander Nevsky," the ballet "Romeo and Juliet," and the orchestral pieces

"Classical Symphony," "Suite from Lieutenant Kije," "Scythian Suite" and "Peter and the Wolf."

Puccini, Giacomo
>BORN: December 22, 1858—Lucca, Italy
>DIED: November 29, 1924—Brussels, Belgium
>HISTORICAL PERIOD: Late Romantic
>COMPOSITIONAL MEDIA: Opera, orchestra, chamber music, organ, choral, songs.
>IMPORTANT ITEMS: Notable works include the operas "Madama Butterfly," "La Boheme" and "Tosca."

Purcell, Henry
>BORN: 1659—London
>DIED: November 21, 1695—Dean's Yard, Westminster, England
>HISTORICAL PERIOD: Baroque
>COMPOSITIONAL MEDIA: Choral, orchestra, chamber music, keyboard, opera, songs, theatrical.
>IMPORTANT ITEMS: Notable works include the opera "Dido and Aeneas."

Q

Quantz, Johann Joachim
>BORN: January 30, 1697—Oberscheden, Germany
>DIED: July 12, 1773—Potsdam, Germany
>HISTORICAL PERIOD: Late Baroque
>COMPOSITIONAL MEDIA: Chamber music, choral, songs.
>IMPORTANT ITEMS: Professional flutist, composer and author. Notable works include numerous compositions for flute.

R

Rachmaninov, Sergei Vassilievich
>BORN: April 1, 1873—Semyonouo, Russia
>DIED: March 28, 1943—Beverly Hills, CA
>HISTORICAL PERIOD: Late Romantic
>COMPOSITIONAL GENRE(S) Keyboard, orchestra, chamber music, choral, opera, songs.
>IMPORTANT ITEMS: Professional pianist, conductor and composer who settled in the United States in 1939. Notable works include the "Piano Concerto No. 2," "Isle of the Dead" for orchestra, "Rhapsody on a Theme of Paganini" for piano and orchestra and the "Prelude in C sharp minor" for solo piano.

Rameau, Jean-Philippe
>BORN: September 25, 1683—Dijon, France
>DIED: September 12, 1764—Paris
>HISTORICAL PERIOD: Baroque
>COMPOSITIONAL MEDIA: Ballet, opera, chamber music, keyboard, choral.
>IMPORTANT ITEMS: Organist, composer and music theorist best known for his text book on harmony "Traité de l'harmonie."

Raposo, Joseph G.
> BORN: February 8, 1937—Fall River, MA
> DIED: February 5, 1989—Bronxville, NY
> HISTORICAL PERIOD: Modern (Popular)
> COMPOSITIONAL GENRE(S) Popular songs, TV.
> IMPORTANT ITEM(S) Notable songs include those written for children's TV programs including "The Electric Company," "The Muppet Show" and "Sesame Street."

Ravel, (Joseph) Maurice
> BORN: March 7, 1875—Ciboure, France
> DIED: December 28, 1937—Paris
> HISTORICAL PERIOD: Modern
> COMPOSITIONAL MEDIA: Chamber music, orchestra, ballet, keyboard, choral, opera.
> IMPORTANT ITEMS: Important impressionist composer. Notable works include "Pavane pour une Infante défunte," "Rhapsodie espagnole," "Ma Mère L'Oye," "La Valse" and "Bolero."

Read, Gardner
> BORN: January 2, 1913—Evanston, IL
> HISTORICAL PERIOD: Modern
> COMPOSITIONAL MEDIA: Orchestra, chamber music, keyboard, choral, opera, songs.
> IMPORTANT ITEMS: Award-winning composer and author.

Reed, Lou [Louis] (Allen)
> BORN: March 2, 1942—New York
> HISTORICAL PERIOD: Modern (Popular)
> COMPOSITIONAL MEDIA: Popular songs.
> IMPORTANT ITEMS: Guitarist, singer and songwriter whose notable songs include "Walk on the Wild Side."

Reger, (Johann Baptist Joseph) Max [Maximillian]
> BORN: March 19, 1873—Brand, Bavaria
> DIED: May 11, 1916—Leipzig, Germany
> HISTORICAL PERIOD: Late Romantic
> COMPOSITIONAL MEDIA: Orchestra, chamber music, keyboard, choral.
> IMPORTANT ITEMS: Notable works include "Variations and Fugue on a Theme By Mozart."

Reich, Steve [Stephan] (Michael)
> BORN: October 3, 1936—New York
> HISTORICAL PERIOD: Modern
> COMPOSITIONAL MEDIA: Chamber music, electronic, orchestra.
> IMPORTANT ITEMS: Compositions are in the minimalist style.

Reicha, Antoine [Antonin or Anton] (-Joseph)
> BORN: February 26, 1770—Prague
> DIED: May 28, 1836—Paris
> HISTORICAL PERIOD: Classical
> COMPOSITIONAL MEDIA: Chamber music, orchestra.
>
> IMPORTANT ITEMS: Notable works include numerous chamber music compositions for wind instruments.

Reinecke, Carl (Heinrich Carsten)
> BORN: June 23, 1824—Altona, Germany
> DIED: March 10, 1910—Leipzig, Germany
> HISTORICAL PERIOD: Romantic
> COMPOSITIONAL MEDIA: Chamber music, orchestra,

keyboard, choral, opera, songs.
IMPORTANT ITEMS: Professional pianist, conductor, teacher and prolific composer.

Respighi, Ottorino
BORN: July 9, 1879—Bologna, Italy
DIED: April 18, 1936—Rome
HISTORICAL PERIOD: Late Romantic/Modern
COMPOSITIONAL MEDIA: Orchestra, chamber music, opera, ballet, keyboard, choral, songs.
IMPORTANT ITEMS: Notable works include the symphonic poems "The Pines of Rome" and "The Fountains of Rome."

Reynolds, Roger (Lee)
BORN: July 18, 1934—Detroit, MI
HISTORICAL PERIOD: Modern
COMPOSITIONAL MEDIA: Orchestra, chamber music, theater, keyboard, choral, electronic.
IMPORTANT ITEMS: Awarded the Pulitzer Prize in 1989 for "Whispers Out of Time."

Reynolds, Verne (Becker)
BORN: July 18, 1926—Lyons, KS
HISTORICAL PERIOD: Modern
COMPOSITIONAL MEDIA: Chamber music, orchestra, choral, songs, band.
IMPORTANT ITEMS: Professional horn player and composer.

Richard, Keith
[real name: Keith Richards]
BORN: December 18, 1943—Dartford, Kent, England
HISTORICAL PERIOD: Modern (Popular).
COMPOSITIONAL MEDIA: Popular songs.
IMPORTANT ITEMS: Lead guitar player of the rock group The Rolling Stones. Notable songs include "(I Can't Get No) Satisfaction" and "Get Off of My Cloud."

Riegger, Wallingford (Constantin)
BORN: April 29, 1885—Albany, GA
DIED: April 2, 1961—New York
HISTORICAL PERIOD: Modern
COMPOSITIONAL MEDIA: Orchestra, chamber music, ballet, keyboard, choral, songs.
IMPORTANT ITEMS: Prolific composer and teacher whose compositions incorporate twelve-tone techniques.

Rimsky-Korsakov, Nikolai (Andreievich)
BORN: March 18, 1844—Tikhvin, Russia
DIED: June 21, 1908—Liubensk, Russia
HISTORICAL PERIOD: Romantic
COMPOSITIONAL MEDIA: Orchestra, chamber music, opera, keyboard, choral, songs, band.
IMPORTANT ITEMS: Notable works include the symphonic poems "Scheherazade," "Capriccio espagnol" and "Russian Easter Overture."

Rochberg, George
BORN: July 5, 1918—Paterson, NJ
HISTORICAL PERIOD: Modern
COMPOSITIONAL MEDIA: Chamber music, orchestra, keyboard, choral, songs, opera, band.
IMPORTANT ITEMS: Compositions incorporate twelve-tone techniques and quotations of other composers works.

Rodgers, Richard (Charles)
>BORN: June 28, 1902—Long Island, NY
>DIED: December 30, 1979—New York
>HISTORICAL PERIOD: Modern (Popular)
>COMPOSITIONAL MEDIA: Popular songs, musicals.
>IMPORTANT ITEMS: Notable works include the Broadway musicals "Oklahoma" (awarded the Pulitzer Prize in 1944), "Carousel," "South Pacific" (awarded the Pulitzer Prize in 1950), "The King and I," "Flower Drum Song" and "The Sound of Music."

Rodrigo, Joaquín
>BORN: November 22, 1901—Sagunto, Valencia, Spain
>HISTORICAL PERIOD: Modern
>COMPOSITIONAL MEDIA: Orchestra, chamber music, ballet, keyboard, guitar.
>IMPORTANT ITEMS: Became blind as a child. Notable works include "Concierto de Aranjuez" for guitar and orchesta.

Rorem, Ned
>BORN: October 23, 1923—Richmond, IN
>HISTORICAL PERIOD: Modern
>COMPOSITIONAL MEDIA: Orchestra, songs, chamber music, keyboard, choral, opera.
>IMPORTANT ITEMS: Awarded the Pulitzer Prize in 1976 for "Air Music." He is considered the foremost American composer of songs.

Rossini, Gioacchino (Antonio)
>BORN: February 29, 1792—Pesaro, Italy
>DIED: November 13, 1868—Paris
>HISTORICAL PERIOD: Late Classical
>COMPOSITIONAL MEDIA: Opera, orchestra, chamber music, keyboard, choral, songs.
>IMPORTANT ITEMS: Notable works include the operas "William Tell," "La Cenerentola" and "Il Barbiere de Siviglia" (The Barber of Seville).

Rota (Rinaldi), Nino
>BORN: December 3, 1911—Milan
>DIED: April 10, 1979—Rome
>HISTORICAL PERIOD: Modern
>COMPOSITIONAL MEDIA: Film, opera, orchestra, ballet, choral, chamber music, keyboard.
>IMPORTANT ITEMS: Notable works include the soundtracks to the films "Fellini's 8½" and "The Godfather" parts 1 & 2.

Roussel, Albert (Charles Paul Marie)
>BORN: April 5, 1869—Tourcoing, France
>DIED: August 23, 1937—Royan, France
>HISTORICAL PERIOD: Late Romantic/Modern
>COMPOSITIONAL MEDIA: Orchestra, chamber music, opera, ballet, keyboard, songs.
>IMPORTANT ITEMS: Compositions are in a neo-classical style. Notable works include the ballet "Bacchus et Ariane."

Rózsa, Miklós
>BORN: April 18, 1907—Budapest
>DIED: July 27, 1995—Los Angeles
>HISTORICAL PERIOD: Modern
>COMPOSITIONAL MEDIA: Film, orchestra, chamber music, choral, songs.
>IMPORTANT ITEMS: Notable works include the score for the film "Ben-Hur."

Rubinstein, Anton (Grigorievich)
    BORN: November 28, 1829—Vykhvatinetz, Russia
    DIED: November 20, 1894—Peterhof, Russia
    HISTORICAL PERIOD: Romantic
    COMPOSITIONAL MEDIA: Keyboard, opera, orchestra, chamber music, choral, songs.
    IMPORTANT ITEMS: Professional pianist and prolific composer.

Ruggles, Carl (Charles Sprague)
    BORN: March 11, 1876—Marion, MA
    DIED: October 24, 1971—Bennington, VT
    HISTORICAL PERIOD: Modern
    COMPOSITIONAL MEDIA: Orchestra, choral, chamber music, keyboard, songs.
    IMPORTANT ITEMS: Professional violinist, composer, teacher and painter. Compositions are dissonant and atonal.

S

Saint-Saëns, (Charles-) Camille
    BORN: October 9, 1835—Paris
    DIED: December 16, 1921—Algiers
    HISTORICAL PERIOD: Romantic
    COMPOSITIONAL MEDIA: Orchestra, chamber music, ballet, keyboard, choral, opera, songs.
    IMPORTANT ITEMS: Prolific composer whose notable works include "Carnival of the Animals" and the opera "Samson et Dalila."

Salieri, Antonio
    BORN: August 18, 1750—Verona, Italy
    DIED: May 7, 1825—Vienna
    HISTORICAL PERIOD: Classical
    COMPOSITIONAL MEDIA: Opera, orchestra, chamber music, keyboard, choral.
    IMPORTANT ITEMS: Prolific composer, conductor and teacher whose students included Beethoven, Schubert and Liszt.

Salonen, Esa-Pekka
    BORN: June 30, 1958—Helsinki
    HISTORICAL PERIOD: Modern
    COMPOSITIONAL MEDIA: Orchestra, chamber music, keyboard.
    IMPORTANT ITEMS: In addition to composing, he was appointed music director of the Los Angeles Philharmonic in 1992.

Salzédo, (Leon) Carlos
    BORN: April 6, 1885—Arcachon, France
    DIED: August 17, 1961—Waterville, ME
    HISTORICAL PERIOD: Modern
    COMPOSITIONAL MEDIA: Orchestra, chamber music.
    IMPORTANT ITEMS: Professional harpist, composer, author and teacher. All compositions include the harp. Introduced special effects for the harp.

Sammartini, Giovanni Battista
    BORN: c. 1700—Milan
    DIED: January 15, 1775—Milan
    HISTORICAL PERIOD: Early Classical
    COMPOSITIONAL MEDIA: Symphony, chamber

music, opera, choral.
IMPORTANT ITEMS: Very prolific composer and teacher of Gluck.

Satie, Erik (Alfred-Leslie)
BORN: May 17, 1866—Honfleur, France
DIED: July 1, 1925—Paris
HISTORICAL PERIOD: Modern
COMPOSITIONAL MEDIA: Keyboard, orchestra, ballet, choral, theatrical.
IMPORTANT ITEMS: Influential composer whose most notable works include the "Gymnopédie" for solo piano.

Scarlatti, (Pietro) Alessandro (Gaspare)
BORN: May 2, 1660—Palermo, Italy
DIED: October 22, 1725—Naples, Italy
HISTORICAL PERIOD: Baroque
COMPOSITIONAL MEDIA: Opera, choral, chamber music, keyboard.
IMPORTANT ITEMS: Founder of the Neopolitan school and prolific composer who helped develop the opera. Father of Domenico Scarlatti.

Scarlatti, (Giuseppe) Domenico
BORN: October 26, 1685—Naples, Italy
DIED: July 23, 1757—Madrid
HISTORICAL PERIOD: Late Baroque
COMPOSITIONAL GENRE(S): Keyboard, choral, opera.
IMPORTANT ITEMS: Prolific and important composer of keyboard (especially harpsichord) music. Son of Alesandro Scarlatti.

Scheidt, Samuel
BORN: November 3, 1587—Halle, Germany
DIED: March 24, 1654—Halle, Germany
HISTORICAL PERIOD: Early Baroque
COMPOSITIONAL MEDIA: Keyboard, choral, chamber music.
IMPORTANT ITEMS: Professional organist, teacher and composer best known for his organ and choral music.

Schein, Johann Hermann
BORN: January 20, 1586—Grünhain, Saxony
DIED: November 19, 1630—Leipzig, Germany
HISTORICAL PERIOD: Baroque
COMPOSITIONAL MEDIA: Choral, chamber music.
IMPORTANT ITEMS: Prolific composer who brought an Italian influence to German music. Notable works include numerous choral compositions.

Schnabel, Artur
BORN: April 17, 1882—Lipnik, Austria
DIED: August 15, 1951—Axenstein, Switzerland
HISTORICAL PERIOD: Modern
COMPOSITIONAL GENRE(S): Orchestra, chamber music, keyboard, songs.
IMPORTANT ITEMS: Professional pianist and composer whose works are dissonant and atonal.

Schoenberg, Arnold (Franz Walter)
BORN: September 13, 1874—Vienna
DIED: July 13, 1951—Los Angeles
HISTORICAL PERIOD: Modern
COMPOSITIONAL MEDIA: Orchestra, chamber music, keyboard, choral, opera, songs, band.

IMPORTANT ITEMS: Influential composer and teacher who originated the twelve-tone technique. Pupils include Berg and Webern. Notable works include "Verklärte Nacht" for strings, "Five Piano Pieces" Op.23 and "Pierrot lunaire" for voice and instruments.

Schubert, Franz (Peter)
BORN: January 31, 1797—Vienna
DIED: November 19, 1828—Vienna
HISTORICAL PERIOD: Early Romantic
COMPOSITIONAL MEDIA: Songs, orchestra, chamber music, keyboard, choral, opera.
IMPORTANT ITEMS: Highly prolific and important composer. Notable works include the "Unfinished" and "Great C Major" symphonies, six Masses, numerous chamber and piano pieces, and a large number of brilliant songs including "Gretchen am Spinnrade," "Erlkönig" and the song cycles "Die schöne Müllerin" and "Die Winterreise."

Schuller, Gunther (Alexander)
BORN: November 22, 1925—New York
HISTORICAL PERIOD: Modern
COMPOSITIONAL MEDIA: Orchestra, chamber music, ballet, keyboard, choral, opera, songs, band, film, TV.
IMPORTANT ITEMS: Compositions incorporate jazz and serial techniques.

Schuman, William
BORN: August 4, 1910—New York
DIED: February 15, 1992—New York
HISTORICAL PERIOD: Modern
COMPOSITIONAL MEDIA: Orchestra, chamber music, keyboard, choral, opera, songs, band.
IMPORTANT ITEMS: Awarded the Pulitzer Prize in 1943 for "A Free Song" and again in 1985. Compositions are melodic and contain elements of jazz.

Schumann, Clara Josephine [maiden name: Wieck]
BORN: September 13, 1819—Leipzig, Germany
DIED: May 20, 1896—Frankfurt, Germany
HISTORICAL PERIOD: Romantic
COMPOSITIONAL MEDIA: Keyboard, chamber music, orchestra, songs.
IMPORTANT ITEMS: Professional pianist, teacher and talented composer. Wife of Robert Schumann.

Schumann, Robert (Alexander)
BORN: June 8, 1810—Zwickau, Saxony
DIED: July 29, 1856—Endenich, Germany
HISTORICAL PERIOD: Romantic
COMPOSITIONAL MEDIA: Orchestra, chamber music, keyboard, choral, songs, opera.
IMPORTANT ITEMS: Professional pianist, author and prolific composer. Notable works include four symphonies, a piano concerto, chamber music and numerous pieces for solo piano including "Papillons" and "Kinderscenen" (Scenes from Childhood).

Schütz, Heinrich
BORN: October 8, 1585—Köstritz, Germany
DIED: November 6, 1672—Dresden
HISTORICAL PERIOD: Baroque
COMPOSITIONAL MEDIA: Choral, chamber music, opera, songs.

IMPORTANT ITEMS: Significant composer who adapted Italian styles to German music. He composed the first German opera "Dafne" (which is now lost) and numerous sacred choral works.

Scriabin, Alexander (Nikolaievich)
BORN: January 6, 1872—Moscow
DIED: April 27, 1915—Moscow
HISTORICAL PERIOD: Late Romantic/Modern
COMPOSITIONAL MEDIA: Keyboard, orchestra, chamber music.
IMPORTANT ITEMS: Virtuoso pianist and composer whose compositions are harmonically daring.

Sessions, Roger (Huntington)
BORN: December 28, 1896—Brooklyn, NY
DIED: March 16, 1985—Princeton, NJ
HISTORICAL PERIOD: Modern
COMPOSITIONAL MEDIA: Orchestra, chamber music, keyboard, choral, opera, songs.
IMPORTANT ITEMS: Influential composer and teacher. Compositions are usually atonal and later works incorporated serial techniques.

Shostakovich, Dmitri (Dmitrievich)
BORN: September 25, 1906—St. Petersburg
DIED: August 9, 1975—Moscow
HISTORICAL PERIOD: Modern
COMPOSITIONAL MEDIA: Orchestra, choral, chamber music, ballet, keyboard, opera, songs, film.
IMPORTANT ITEMS: Notable works include 15 symphonies, the operas "The Nose" and "The Lady Macbeth of the Mtsensk" and the ballet "The Age of Gold."

Sibelius, Jean [Johan Julius Christian]
BORN: December 8, 1865—Hämeenlinna, Finland
DIED: September 20, 1957—Järvenpää, Finland
HISTORICAL PERIOD: Romantic
COMPOSITIONAL MEDIA: Orchestra, chamber music, keyboard, choral, opera, songs.
IMPORTANT ITEMS: Composed nationalistic Finnish music. Notable works include the orchestral works "The Swan of Tuonela" and "Finlandia."

Siegmeister, Elie
BORN: January 15, 1909—New York
DIED: March 10, 1991—Manhasset, NY
HISTORICAL PERIOD: Modern
COMPOSITIONAL MEDIA: Orchestra, choral, chamber music, keyboard, opera, songs.
IMPORTANT ITEMS: Prolific composer, conductor, pianist and teacher.

Simon, Paul
BORN: October 13, 1941—Newark, NJ
HISTORICAL PERIOD: Modern (Popular).
COMPOSITIONAL MEDIA: Popular songs.
IMPORTANT ITEMS: After a successful partnership with Art Garfunkel (Simon and Garfunkel) he continued with a successful solo career. Notable works include "The Sound of Silence" and "Graceland."

Slonimsky, Nicolas [Nikolai] (Leonidovich)
BORN: April 27, 1894—St. Petersburg
DIED: December 25, 1995—Los Angeles
HISTORICAL PERIOD: Modern
COMPOSITIONAL MEDIA: Orchestra, chamber music,

keyboard, songs.
IMPORTANT ITEMS: Compositions incorporate polytonality, atonality and quarter-tone techniques. Known as a well-respected author and lecturer.

Smetana, Bedřich
BORN: March 2, 1824—Leitomischl, Bohemia
DIED: May 12, 1884—Prague
HISTORICAL PERIOD: Romantic
COMPOSITIONAL MEDIA: Orchestra, chamber music, keyboard, choral, opera, songs.
IMPORTANT ITEMS: Notable works include the opera "The Bartered Bride," the symphonic poem "Ma Vlast" and the string quartet "From My Life."

Smith, Hale
BORN: June 29, 1925—Cleveland, OH
HISTORICAL PERIOD: Modern
COMPOSITIONAL MEDIA: Orchestra, chamber music, keyboard, choral, songs, band.
IMPORTANT ITEMS: Compositions incorporate serial techniques and jazz.

Soler, Antonio
BORN: December 3, 1729—Olot, Spain
DIED: December 20, 1783—El Escorial, Spain
HISTORICAL PERIOD: Late Baroque
COMPOSITIONAL MEDIA: Choral, chamber music, keyboard.
IMPORTANT ITEMS: Notable works include "Fandango" for keyboard.

Sondheim, Stephen (Joshua)
BORN: March 22, 1930—New York
HISTORICAL PERIOD: Modern (Popular)
COMPOSITIONAL MEDIA: Popular songs, musicals.
IMPORTANT ITEMS: Composer and lyricist whose notable works include the Broadway musicals "Company," "A Little Night Music" and "Sunday in the Park With George."

Sor [Sors], Fernando
BORN: February 13, 1778—Barcelona
DIED: July 10, 1839—Paris
HISTORICAL PERIOD: Classical
COMPOSITIONAL MEDIA: Guitar, ballet, chamber music, opera, orchestra.
IMPORTANT ITEMS: Notable for his method and works for guitar.

Sousa, John Philip
BORN: November 6, 1854—Washington, DC
DIED: March 6, 1932—Reading, PA
HISTORICAL PERIOD: Late Romantic (Popular)
COMPOSITIONAL MEDIA: Band, opera, orchestra, chamber music, songs, choral.
IMPORTANT ITEMS: Considered "The March King." Notable marches include "The Stars and Stripes Forever," "El Capitan," "The Liberty Bell," "Nobles of the Mystic Shrine," "The Washington Post" and "Semper Fidelis."

Sowerby, Leo
BORN: May 1, 1895—Grand Rapids, MI
DIED: July 7, 1968—Port Clinton, OH
HISTORICAL PERIOD: Modern
COMPOSITIONAL MEDIA: Orchestra, chamber music, keyboard, choral, songs.

IMPORTANT ITEMS: Awarded the Pulitzer Prize in 1946 for "Canticle of the Sun."

Spohr, Ludwig [Ludewig]
BORN: April 5, 1784—Braunschweig, Germany
DIED: October 22, 1859—Kassel, Germany
HISTORICAL PERIOD: Early Romantic
COMPOSITIONAL MEDIA: Orchestra, chamber music, opera, keyboard, choral, songs.
IMPORTANT ITEMS: Professional violinist and composer.

Stamitz, Johann Wenzel Anton
BORN: June 19, 1717—Deutsch-Brod, Bohemia
DIED: March 27, 1757—Mannheim, Germany
HISTORICAL PERIOD: Late Baroque/Early Classical
COMPOSITIONAL MEDIA: Orchestra, chamber music.
IMPORTANT ITEMS: Professional violinist and prolific composer who influenced Haydn and Mozart. Father of Carl Philipp Stamitz.

Stamitz, Carl Philipp
BORN: May 7, 1745—Mannheim, Germany
DIED: November 9, 1801—Jena, Germany
HISTORICAL PERIOD: Classical
COMPOSITIONAL MEDIA: Orchestra, chamber music, choral, opera.
IMPORTANT ITEMS: Professional violinist and prolific composer.

Starer, Robert
BORN: January 8, 1924—Vienna
HISTORICAL PERIOD: Modern
COMPOSITIONAL MEDIA: Orchestra, chamber music, ballet, opera, keyboard, choral, songs.
IMPORTANT ITEMS: Award-winning composer, teacher and author. Became a citizen of the United States in 1957.

Stevens, Halsey
BORN: December 3, 1908—Scott, NY
DIED: January 20, 1989—Long Beach, CA
HISTORICAL PERIOD: Modern
COMPOSITIONAL MEDIA: Orchestra, chamber music, keyboard, songs.
IMPORTANT ITEMS: Prolific composer and teacher. Chairman of the music department at the University of Southern California from 1948–1976.

Still, William Grant
BORN: May 11, 1895—Woodville, MS
DIED: December 3, 1978—Los Angeles
HISTORICAL PERIOD: Modern
COMPOSITIONAL MEDIA: Orchestra, chamber music, ballet, keyboard, choral, opera, songs, band.
IMPORTANT ITEMS: Compositions incorporate American folk songs. Notable works include the "Afro-American Symphony."

Stockhausen, Karlheinz
BORN: August 22, 1928—Mödrath, Germany
HISTORICAL PERIOD: Modern
COMPOSITIONAL MEDIA: Orchestra, chamber music, keyboard, choral, electronic.
IMPORTANT ITEMS: Compositions incorporate graphic notation and serial, aleatory, spatial and electronic techniques.

Stradella, Alessandro
> BORN: c. 1639—Nepi, Italy
> DIED: February 25, 1682—Genoa, Italy
> HISTORICAL PERIOD: Baroque
> COMPOSITIONAL MEDIA: Opera, chamber music, choral.
> IMPORTANT ITEMS: Numerous operas were written about his life and murder.

Strauss, Jr., Johann
> BORN: October 25, 1825—Vienna
> DIED: June 3, 1899—Vienna
> HISTORICAL PERIOD: Romantic
> COMPOSITIONAL MEDIA: Orchestra, operetta.
> IMPORTANT ITEMS: Considered "The Waltz King." Notable works include the waltzes "The Blue Danube," "Wine Women and Song" and "Tales from the Vienna Woods," and the operetta "Die Fledermaus." Son of Johann Strauss, Sr.

Strauss, Sr., Johann
> BORN: March 14, 1804—Vienna
> DIED: September 25, 1849—Vienna
> HISTORICAL PERIOD: Romantic
> COMPOSITIONAL MEDIA: Orchestra.
> IMPORTANT ITEMS: Composer of numerous waltzes and other dances. The father of Johann Strauss, Jr.

Strauss, Richard (Georg)
> BORN: June 11, 1864—Munich, Germany
> DIED: September 8, 1949—Garmisch-Partenkirchen, Germany
> HISTORICAL PERIOD: Late Romantic
> COMPOSITIONAL MEDIA: Orchestra, opera, chamber music, ballet, keyboard, choral, songs.
> IMPORTANT ITEMS: Prolific composer and conductor. Notable works include the tone poems "Till Eulenspiegel's Merry Pranks," "Also Sprach Zarathustra" and "Don Juan" and the operas "Salome," "Der Rosenkavalier" and "Elektra."

Stravinsky, Igor (Feodorovich)
> BORN: June 17, 1882—Oranienbaum, Russia
> DIED: April 6, 1971—New York
> HISTORICAL PERIOD: Modern
> COMPOSITIONAL MEDIA: Orchestra, ballet, chamber music, keyboard, choral, opera, songs.
> IMPORTANT ITEMS: One of the most important composers of the 20th century. He settled in the U.S. in 1939. Compositions incorporate many techniques including extreme dissonance, jazz, bitonality and serial techniques. Notable works include the "Symphony of Psalms" and the ballets "The Firebird" "Petrushka," and "The Rite of Spring."

Strayhorn, Billy
> BORN: November 29, 1915—Dayton, OH
> DIED: May 31, 1967—New York
> HISTORICAL PERIOD: Modern (Popular)
> COMPOSITIONAL MEDIA: Popular songs, jazz.
> IMPORTANT ITEMS: Professional jazz pianist, arranger and composer. Co-wrote many of Duke Ellington's works including "Take the A Train."

Styne, Jule
> BORN: December 31, 1905—London
> HISTORICAL PERIOD: Modern (Popular)
> COMPOSITIONAL GENRE(S): Popular songs, musicals, film.
> IMPORTANT ITEMS: Notable works include the Broadway musicals "Gentlemen Prefer Blondes," "Gypsy" and "Funny Girl."

Subotnick, Morton
> BORN: April 14, 1933—Los Angeles
> HISTORICAL PERIOD: Modern
> COMPOSITIONAL MEDIA: Orchestra, chamber music, electronic.
> IMPORTANT ITEMS: Compositions incorporate electronic, mixed media and tape techniques.

Suk, Josef
> BORN: January 4, 1874—Křečovice
> DIED: May 29, 1935—Benešov, near Prague
> HISTORICAL PERIOD: Late Romantic
> COMPOSITIONAL GENRE(S): Orchestra, chamber music, keyboard, choral.
> IMPORTANT ITEMS: Early compositions influenced by Dvořák but later works were harmonically daring, almost atonal.

Sullivan, Sir Arthur (Seymour)
> BORN: May 13, 1842—London
> DIED: November 22, 1900—London
> HISTORICAL PERIOD: Romantic
> COMPOSITIONAL MEDIA: Operettas, orchestra, chamber music, ballet, choral, songs.
> IMPORTANT ITEMS: Notable works include the popular operettas "H.M.S. Pinafore," "The Pirates of Penzance" and "The Mikado."

Suppe, Franz von
> BORN: April 18, 1819—Spalato, Dalmatia
> DIED: May 21, 1895—Vienna
> HISTORICAL PERIOD: Romantic
> COMPOSITIONAL MEDIA: Operettas, orchestra, chamber music, choral, opera, songs.
> IMPORTANT ITEMS: Notable works include the "Poet and Peasant" overture.

Süssmayr, Franz Xaver
> BORN: 1766—Schwanenstadt, Austria
> DIED: September 17, 1803—Vienna
> HISTORICAL PERIOD: Classical
> COMPOSITIONAL MEDIA: Opera, orchestra, chamber music, choral.
> IMPORTANT ITEMS: Best known for completing Mozart's unfinished Requiem.

Sweelinck, Jan Pieterszoon
> BORN: 1562—Deventer, Netherlands
> DIED: October 16, 1621—Amsterdam
> HISTORICAL PERIOD: Renaissance
> COMPOSITIONAL MEDIA: Keyboard, choral.
> IMPORTANT ITEMS: The first composer to use the pedals of the organ as an independent part in a fugue.

T

Tailleferre [Taillefesse], (Marcelle) Germaine
BORN: April 19, 1892—Parc-Saint-Maur, France
DIED: November 7, 1983—Paris
HISTORICAL PERIOD: Modern
COMPOSITIONAL MEDIA: Orchestra, chamber music, ballet, keyboard, choral, opera, songs, theatrical, film.
IMPORTANT ITEMS: The only female member of Les Six.

Takemitsu, Toru
BORN: October 8, 1930—Tokyo
DIED: February 20, 1996—Tokyo
HISTORICAL PERIOD: Modern
COMPOSITIONAL MEDIA: Orchestral, choral, chamber music, electronic, keyboard.
IMPORTANT ITEMS: Combined Eastern and Western compositional styles and philosophies.

Tallis, Thomas
BORN: c. 1505
DIED: November 23, 1585—Greenwich, England
HISTORICAL PERIOD: Renaissance
COMPOSITIONAL GENRE(S): Choral, keyboard, chamber music.
IMPORTANT ITEMS: One of the finest composers of his time. Notable works include the 40-part motet "Spem in alium."

Tartini, Giuseppe
BORN: April 8, 1692—Pirano, Istria
DIED: February 26, 1770—Padua, Italy
HISTORICAL PERIOD: Baroque
COMPOSITIONAL MEDIA: Orchestra, chamber music, choral.
IMPORTANT ITEMS: Professional violinist and prolific composer best known for his violin music. Notable works include the "Devil's Trill" sonata for violin.

Tchaikovsky, Piotr Ilyich
BORN: May 7, 1840—Votkinsk, Russia
DIED: November 6, 1893—St. Petersburg
HISTORICAL PERIOD: Romantic
COMPOSITIONAL MEDIA: Orchestra, chamber music, opera, ballet, keyboard, choral, songs.
IMPORTANT ITEMS: Notable works include "Symphony No. 6" (Pathetique), the ballets "Swan Lake" and the "Nutcracker," and the orchestral works "Romeo and Juliet," "1812 Overture" and "Capriccio Italien."

Tcherepnin, Alexander (Nikolaievich)
BORN: January 20, 1899—St. Petersburg
DIED: September 29, 1977—Paris
HISTORICAL PERIOD: Modern
COMPOSITIONAL MEDIA: Orchestra, chamber music, ballet, keyboard, opera, choral, songs.
IMPORTANT ITEMS: Professional pianist, conductor and composer whose music explores European and oriental folk music.

Telemann, Georg Philipp
BORN: March 14, 1681—Magdeburg, Germany
DIED: June 25, 1767—Hamburg, Germany
HISTORICAL PERIOD: Late Baroque/Early Classical
COMPOSITIONAL MEDIA: Opera, choral, chamber

music, orchestra, keyboard.
IMPORTANT ITEMS: Professional organist and prolific composer who composed in the gallant style.

Thompson, Randall
BORN: April 21, 1899—New York
DIED: July 9, 1984—Boston, MA
HISTORICAL PERIOD: Modern
COMPOSITIONAL MEDIA: Choral, orchestra, chamber music, keyboard, opera, songs.
IMPORTANT ITEMS: Award-winning composer and teacher. Notable works include numerous choral works and the successful "2nd Symphony."

Thomson, Virgil (Garnett)
BORN: November 25, 1896—Kansas City, MO
DIED: September 30,1989—New York
HISTORICAL PERIOD: Modern
COMPOSITIONAL MEDIA: Orchestra, chamber music, film, ballet, keyboard, choral, opera, songs.
IMPORTANT ITEMS: Awarded the Pulitzer Prize in 1948 for the film score "Louisiana Story." Notable works include the opera "Four Saints in Three Acts" and the film score "The Plough That Broke the Plains."

Tippett, Sir Michael (Kemp)
BORN: January 2, 1905—London
HISTORICAL PERIOD: Modern
COMPOSITIONAL MEDIA: Orchestra, choral, chamber music, opera, keyboard, songs.
IMPORTANT ITEMS: Notable works include the opera "King Priam."

Toch, Ernst
BORN: December 7, 1887—Vienna
DIED: October 1, 1964—Los Angeles
HISTORICAL PERIOD: Modern
COMPOSITIONAL MEDIA: Orchestra, chamber music, choral, keyboard, opera, songs, film.
IMPORTANT ITEMS: Award-winning composer and author who settled in the United States in 1934. Awarded the Pulitzer Prize in 1956 for his "Third Symphony."

Torelli, Giuseppe
BORN: April 22, 1658—Verona, Italy
DIED: February 8, 1709—Bologna, Italy
HISTORICAL PERIOD: Baroque
COMPOSITIONAL MEDIA: Orchestra, chamber music, choral.
IMPORTANT ITEMS: Professional violinist and one of the first composers of the concerto grosso.

Townshend, Pete [Peter] (Dennis Blandford)
BORN: May 19, 1945—Chiswick, England
HISTORICAL PERIOD: Modern (Popular).
COMPOSITIONAL MEDIA: Popular songs.
IMPORTANT ITEMS: Singer, guitarist and songwriter for the group The Who. Notable works include the songs "My Generation" and the rock opera "Tommy."

Torke, Michael
BORN: September 22, 1961—Milwaukee, WI
HISTORICAL PERIOD: Modern
COMPOSITIONAL MEDIA: Orchestra, chamber music, keyboard, choral, opera, ballet.
IMPORTANT ITEMS: Award winning composer and pianist. Compositions incorporate rock, jazz and classical styles.

Tudor, David (Eugene)
BORN: January 20, 1926—Philadelphia, PA
HISTORICAL PERIOD: Modern
COMPOSITIONAL MEDIA: Chamber music, ballet, electronic.
IMPORTANT ITEMS: Pioneer in electronic music techniques.

Türk, Daniel Gottlob
BORN: August 10, 1750—Clausnitz, Saxony
DIED: August 26, 1813—Halle, Germany
HISTORICAL PERIOD: Classical
COMPOSITIONAL MEDIA: Choral, keyboard, orchestra, opera, songs.
IMPORTANT ITEMS: Notable works include keyboard and choral compositions.

U

Ussachevsky, Vladimir (Alexis)
BORN: November 3, 1911—Hailar, Manchuria
DIED: January 2, 1990—New York
HISTORICAL PERIOD: Modern
COMPOSITIONAL MEDIA: Electronic, chamber music, orchestra, keyboard, choral, film, radio, TV.
IMPORTANT ITEMS: Settled in the United States in 1930. Compositions incorporate electronic and tape techniques. Collaborated with Otto Luening.

V

Van Heusen, Jimmy
[real name: Edward Chester Babcock]
BORN: January 26, 1913—Syracuse, NY
HISTORICAL PERIOD: Modern (Popular)
COMPOSITIONAL MEDIA: Popular songs, film, TV.
IMPORTANT ITEMS: Notable songs include "High Hopes," "Swingin' on a Star" and "Love and Marriage."

Varèse, Edgard (Victor Achille Charles)
BORN: December 22, 1883—Paris
DIED: November 6, 1965—New York
HISTORICAL PERIOD: Modern
COMPOSITIONAL MEDIA: Orchestra, chamber music, choral, electronic.
IMPORTANT ITEMS: Settled in New York in 1915. Notable works include "Ionisation" for percussion orchestra.

Vaughan Williams, Ralph
BORN: October 12, 1872—Down Ampney, England
DIED: August 26, 1958—London
HISTORICAL PERIOD: Late Romantic/Modern
COMPOSITIONAL MEDIA: Orchestra, chamber music, ballet, keyboard, choral, opera, songs, theatrical, film, band.
IMPORTANT ITEMS: Prolific composer of melodic music. Notable works include "3 Norfolk Rhapsodies" and "Fantasia on a Theme by Thomas Tallis."

Verdi, Giuseppe (Fortunino Francesco)
BORN: October 9, 1813—Le Roncole, Italy

DIED: January 27, 1901—Milan, Italy
HISTORICAL PERIOD: Romantic
COMPOSITIONAL MEDIA: Opera, choral, chamber music, songs, keyboard.
IMPORTANT ITEMS: One of the greatest opera composers of all time. Notable works include the "Requiem" and the operas "Rigoletto," "Il Trovatore," "La forza del destino," "La Traviata," "Aida" and "Otello."

Victoria (Vittoria), Tomas Luis de
BORN: c. 1548—Avila, Spain
DIED: August 20, 1611—Madrid
HISTORICAL PERIOD: Late Renaissance
COMPOSITIONAL MEDIA: Choral.
IMPORTANT ITEMS: One of the most important composers of sacred choral music of the late Renaissance.

Villa-Lobos, Heitor
BORN: March 5, 1887—Rio de Janeiro, Brazil
DIED: November 17, 1959—Rio de Janeiro, Brazil
HISTORICAL PERIOD: Modern
COMPOSITIONAL MEDIA: Orchestra, chamber music, keyboard, choral, opera, ballet, songs.
IMPORTANT ITEMS: Prolific composer whose compositions incorporate Brazilian folk music. Notable works include "Bachianas brazileiras No. 5" for soprano voice and eight cellos.

Viotti, Giovanni Battista
BORN: May 12, 1755—Fontanetto da Po, Italy
DIED: March 3, 1824—London
HISTORICAL PERIOD: Classical
COMPOSITIONAL MEDIA: Orchestra, chamber music, keyboard.
IMPORTANT ITEMS: Professional violinist and composer.

Vivaldi, Antonio (Lucio)
BORN: March 4, 1678—Venice
DIED: July 28, 1741—Vienna
HISTORICAL PERIOD: Late Baroque
COMPOSITIONAL MEDIA: Orchestra, opera, chamber music, choral.
IMPORTANT ITEMS: Prolific composer best remembered for "The Four Seasons" for solo violin and strings.

W

Wagner, (Wilhelm) Richard
BORN: May 22, 1813—Leipzig, Germany
DIED: February 13, 1883—Venice
HISTORICAL PERIOD: Late Romantic
COMPOSITIONAL MEDIA: Opera, orchestra, chamber music, keyboard, choral, opera, songs.
IMPORTANT ITEMS: One of the most influential composers of opera who believed that story and music should have equal importance. He called his operas "Music Dramas." Notable operas include "Der fliegende Holländer," "Tannhäuser," "Lohengrin," "Der Ring des Nibelungen," "Tristan und Isolde" and "Die Meistersinger von Nürnberg."

Waldteufel (Lévy), Emil
> BORN: December 9, 1837—Strasbourg, France
> DIED: February 12, 1915—Paris
> HISTORICAL PERIOD: Romantic
> COMPOSITIONAL MEDIA: Orchestral.
> IMPORTANT ITEMS: Composer of numerous waltzes and other dances.

Waller, (Thomas Wright) "Fats"
> BORN: May 21, 1904—New York
> DIED: December 15, 1943—Kansas City, MO
> HISTORICAL PERIOD: Modern (Popular)
> COMPOSITIONAL MEDIA: Musicals, popular songs, jazz.
> IMPORTANT ITEMS: Significant jazz pianist and composer. Notable songs include "Ain't Misbehavin'."

Walton, Sir William (Turner)
> BORN: March 29, 1902—Oldham, England
> DIED: March 8, 1983—Ischia, Italy
> HISTORICAL PERIOD: Modern
> COMPOSITIONAL MEDIA: Orchestra, chamber music, ballet, keyboard, choral, opera, songs, film.
> IMPORTANT ITEMS: Notable works include the chamber piece "Facade" for reciter and 6 instruments, and the oratorio "Belshazzar's Feast."

Ward, Robert
> BORN: September 13, 1917—Cleveland, OH
> HISTORICAL PERIOD: Modern
> COMPOSITIONAL MEDIA: Orchestra, choral, chamber music, keyboard, opera, songs.
> IMPORTANT ITEMS: Awarded the Pulitzer Prize in 1962 for his opera "The Crucible."

Webber, Andrew Lloyd: See Lloyd Webber, Andrew

Weber, Carl Maria (Friedrich Ernst) von
> BORN: November 18, 1786—Eutin, Germany
> DIED: June 5, 1826—London
> HISTORICAL PERIOD: Late Classical/Early Romantic
> COMPOSITIONAL MEDIA: Orchestra, opera, chamber music, keyboard, choral, songs, theatrical.
> IMPORTANT ITEMS: Notable works include the operas "Der Freischütz" and "Oberon."

Webern, Anton (Freidrich Wilhelm von)
> BORN: December 3, 1883—Vienna
> DIED: September 15, 1945—Mittersill, Germany
> HISTORICAL PERIOD: Modern
> COMPOSITIONAL MEDIA: Songs, choral, orchestra, chamber music, keyboard.
> IMPORTANT ITEMS: Compositions incorporate twelve-tone techniques and emphasize tone color. Notable works include "Five Pieces" for orchestra.

Weill, Kurt (Julian)
> BORN: March 2, 1900—Dessau, Germany
> DIED: April 3, 1950—New York
> HISTORICAL PERIOD: Modern
> COMPOSITIONAL MEDIA: Songs, musicals, orchestra, chamber music, keyboard, choral, opera, film.
> IMPORTANT ITEMS: Settled in the United States in 1935. Compositions incorporate jazz, atonal, polyrhythmic and polytonal elements. Notable works include the "Threepenny Opera" which includes the song "Mack the Knife" and the musical play "Lady in the Dark."

Weinberger, Jaromir
BORN: January 8, 1896—Prague
DIED: August 8, 1967—St. Petersburg, FL
HISTORICAL PERIOD: Late Romantic/Modern
COMPOSITIONAL MEDIA: Orchestra, chamber music, keyboard, choral, opera, songs, band.
IMPORTANT ITEMS: Settled in the United States in 1939. Notable works include the polka and fugue from the opera "Schwanda the Bagpiper."

Weisgall, Hugo (David)
BORN: October 13, 1912—Eibenschütz, Moravia
HISTORICAL PERIOD: Modern
COMPOSITIONAL MEDIA: Chamber music, ballet, choral, opera, songs.
IMPORTANT ITEMS: Award winning composer and teacher.

Widor, Charles-Marie
BORN: February 21, 1844—Lyons, France
DIED: March 12, 1937—Paris
HISTORICAL PERIOD: Late Romantic
COMPOSITIONAL MEDIA: Keyboard, opera, ballet, orchestra, choral, chamber music.
IMPORTANT ITEMS: Notable works include 10 organ symphonies.

Willan, Healey
BORN: October 12, 1880—Balham, England
DIED: February 16, 1968—Toronto, Canada
HISTORICAL PERIOD: Modern
COMPOSITIONAL MEDIA: Orchestra, chamber music, keyboard, choral, opera, band, songs, radio.
IMPORTANT ITEMS: Organist, teacher and prolific composer.

Williams Sr., Hank (Hiram)
BORN: September 17, 1923—Georgiana, AL
DIED: January 1, 1953—Oak Hill, VA
HISTORICAL PERIOD: Modern (Popular)
COMPOSITIONAL MEDIA: Popular songs.
IMPORTANT ITEMS: Popular singer, guitarist and songwriter of country music. Notable songs include "Hey, Good Lookin'" and "Move It On Over."

Williams, John (Towner)
BORN: February 8, 1932—New York
HISTORICAL PERIOD: Modern
COMPOSITIONAL MEDIA: Film, orchestra, chamber music.
IMPORTANT ITEMS: Notable film scores include "Jaws," "Star Wars," "ET (The Extraterestrial)," "Close Encounters of the Third Kind," "Jurassic Park" and "Schindler's List."

Wilson, Brian (Douglas)
BORN: June 20, 1942—Hawthorne, CA
HISTORICAL PERIOD: Modern (Popular)
COMPOSITIONAL MEDIA: Popular Songs.
IMPORTANT ITEMS: A member of the surf-music rock group The Beach Boys. Notable songs include "Surfin' USA" and "Help Me Rhonda."

Wolf, Hugo (Filipp Jakob)
BORN: March 13, 1860—Windischgraz, Austria
DIED: February 22, 1903—Vienna
HISTORICAL PERIOD: Late Romantic
COMPOSITIONAL MEDIA: Keyboard, songs, choral,

orchestra, chamber music, opera.
IMPORTANT ITEMS: Notable works include the "Italian Serenade" and numerous lieder.

Wonder, Stevie
 [real name: Steveland Judkins Hardaway]
BORN: May 13, 1951—Saginaw, MI
HISTORICAL PERIOD: Modern (Popular)
COMPOSITIONAL MEDIA: Popular songs, film.
IMPORTANT ITEMS: A significant composer of popular songs. Notable songs include "You Are the Sunshine of My Life," and "I Just Called to Say I Love You."

Wuorinen, Charles
BORN: June 9, 1938—New York
HISTORICAL PERIOD: Modern
COMPOSITIONAL MEDIA: Chamber music, orchestra, keyboard, choral, electronic.
IMPORTANT ITEMS: Compositions incorporate electronic, tape and serial techniques. Awarded the Pulitzer Prize in 1970 for "Time's Encomium" for synthesized sound.

X, Y, Z

Xenakis, Yannis
BORN: May 29, 1922—Braila, Rumania
HISTORICAL PERIOD: Modern
COMPOSITIONAL MEDIA: Chamber music, orchestra, keyboard, ballet, electronic.
IMPORTANT ITEMS: Compositions incorporate aleatory, computer and mathematical techniques.

Young, La Monte (Thornton)
BORN: October 14, 1935—Bern, ID
HISTORICAL PERIOD: Modern
COMPOSITIONAL MEDIA: Chamber music, electronic, keyboard.
IMPORTANT ITEMS: Highly experimental composer.

Zappa, Frank
BORN: December 21, 1940—Baltimore, MD
DIED: December 4, 1993—Los Angeles
HISTORICAL PERIOD: Modern (Popular)
COMPOSITIONAL MEDIA: Popular songs, film, orchestra, choral.
IMPORTANT ITEMS: Best known for popular songs that combined classical and jazz elements.

Zemlinsky, Alexander (Von)
BORN: October 14, 1871—Vienna
DIED: March 15, 1942—Larchmont, NY
HISTORICAL PERIOD: Late Romantic
COMPOSITIONAL MEDIA: Opera, chamber music, orchestra, choral, songs.
IMPORTANT ITEMS: Teacher of Arnold Schoenberg.

Zwilich, Ellen Taaffe
BORN: April 30, 1939—Miami, FL
HISTORICAL PERIOD: Modern
COMPOSITIONAL MEDIA: Orchestra, chamber music, ballet, vocal.
IMPORTANT ITEMS: Awarded the Pulitzer Prize in 1983 for her "Symphony No. 1."